IMAGES
of America
THE CHINESE IN NEVADA

ARRIVAL. The Chinese could each bring a small trunk full of personal items when they arrived from China. An immigration station was established on the San Francisco wharf in a wooden shed until Angel Island, located in the San Francisco Bay, was opened from 1910 to 1940. (National Archives and Records Administration.)

On the Cover: UNKNOWN CHINESE COWBOY. In 1913, a Chinese cowboy dressed in white chaps on a white horse won the rodeo in Elko. Chinese cowboys, although small in number, worked all over Nevada, and most were born in California. (Nevada Historical Society.)

IMAGES
of America

THE CHINESE IN NEVADA

Sue Fawn Chung with
the Nevada State Museum

Copyright © 2011 by Sue Fawn Chung with the Nevada State Museum
ISBN 978-1-5316-4941-8

Published by Arcadia Publishing
Charleston, South Carolina

Library of Congress Control Number: 2010941646

For all general information, please contact Arcadia Publishing:
Telephone 843-853-2070
Fax 843-853-0044
E-mail sales@arcadiapublishing.com
For customer service and orders:
Toll-Free 1-888-313-2665

Visit us on the Internet at www.arcadiapublishing.com

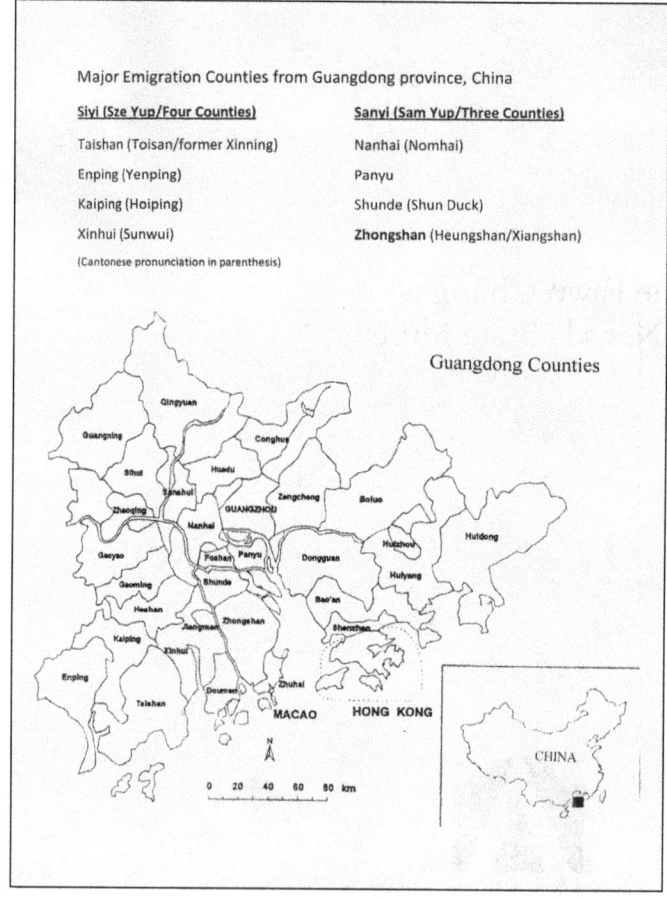

EMIGRATION MAP. Approximately 90 percent of the Chinese immigrating in the 19th century came from three counties in Guangdong: Siyi, Sanyi, and Zhongshan. These counties spoke different dialects of Cantonese that were often unintelligible to each other. Like some European immigrants, many Chinese were a part of chain migration, in which families, kinsmen, and fellow villagers traveled together or followed one another and settled in the same parts of the American West.

CONTENTS

Acknowledgments		6
Introduction		7
1.	Early Mining and Railroad Construction	9
2.	Logging and Later Mining Towns	33
3.	Into the 20th Century	51
4.	Second Generation Chinese and Their Families	61
5.	Reno and Other Towns	79
6.	Entertainment and Later Developments	95
7.	Accomplishments and Contributions	109

ACKNOWLEDGMENTS

The Nevada Humanities, with Judith Winzler as director and funding from the National Endowment for the Humanities, started my interest in collecting images of the Chinese in the United States. Invaluable assistance came from Lee Brumbaugh of the Nevada Historical Society and Robert Nylen of the Nevada State Museum, Carson City. Assistance also came from Peter Michel of the University of Nevada, Las Vegas and Donnelyn Curtis of the University of Nevada, Reno, Special Collections; Claudia Wines of the Northeastern Nevada Museum; Barbara McKay of the Fourth Ward School; Dennis McBride of the Nevada State Museum, Las Vegas; Kate Reeve of the Arizona Historical Society: Central Nevada Historical Society; Dayton Historical Society; and the California Historical Society. I also want to thank staff members of the Oakland Museum, National Archives and Records Administration; National Trust for Historic Preservation; National Forest Service; National Park Service; and other several university libraries, museums, and government archives.

Special thanks go to: Robert Stoldal, Su Kim Chung, Landon Quan, Richard Lym, the Kee family, Fred Frampton, Dale Hom, Robert Morrill, Robert Stoldal, Priscilla Wegars, Maxine Chan, Hilda Matthey's relatives, Della Baker Johns and her family, Theodore and Doris Shoong Lee and their family, Hazel Huey, Peter Yee and his family, Henry Yup, Fred Lee and his family, Kathy Ong, Liane Lee, Esther Louie, and Joan Giannecchini. My husband, Alan, has been invaluable. Without him, this study would not have been possible.

The images in this volume appear courtesy of the Asian American Comparative Collection, Moscow, Idaho (AACC); California Historical Society (CHS); Central Nevada Historical Society, Tonopah (CNHS); Kee Family Collection (Kee); Kline-Morrill Collection (Kline); Richard Lym Collection (Lym); National Archives and Records Administration, San Bruno, California (NARA); Northeastern Nevada Museum, Elko (NENM); Nevada Historical Society, Reno (NHS); National Park Service (NPS); Nevada State Museum, Carson City (NSM); Nevada State Museum, Las Vegas (NSMLV); Kathy Ong (Ong); Theodore and Doris Shoong Lee Collection (Shoong-Lee); University of Nevada, Las Vegas, Lied Library Special Collections (UNLV); Henry Yup (Yup); Nevada State Railroad Museum (NSRM); Su Kim Chung (SK Chung); Robert Stoldal (Stodal); and those fully credited. Unless otherwise noted, the photographs are from the author's private collection.

INTRODUCTION

In 1849, the Chinese in south China heard about the discovery of gold in California. This coincided with a period of economic, social, and political unrest as the weak Manchu rulers of China began to lose their control of China and cheap Western imports, such as cotton cloth, eliminated traditional jobs. Floods, famine, and banditry also contributed to high unemployment. Thousands of Chinese came from Guangdong province in southeastern China in pursuit of instant wealth in "Gold Mountain," the Chinese name for California and often, in general, the United States. They sought new opportunities and a better life.

The two main occupations that attracted them to Nevada were placer mining and railroad work. Around 1855, Mormon settlers invited Chinese laborers to build irrigation ditches for farming and mining and allowed them to settle in Genoa and Johnstown (later called Dayton) to mine. When the rich gold and silver mines of the Comstock (primarily Virginia City and Gold Hill) were discovered in 1859, the Chinese moved there but were prohibited from mining due to local laws. They found opportunities in establishing restaurants, boardinghouses, and laundries, which were primary occupations that employed them into the early 20th century. They operated gaming halls, opium dens, and houses of prostitution. The 1870 census manuscript for Virginia City listed 647 Chinese males and 103 Chinese females with an average age of 23.4 years, but the local press reported about 2,000 Chinese, making it close to the same size as San Francisco's Chinese population. The Chinese traditionally valued land ownership, so the 1861 Nevada Constitution that allowed "alien residents" to own land attracted Chinese associations and wealthy Chinese individuals who purchased property throughout Nevada as well as mining claims outside of the Comstock that Euro American miners, who staked the original claim, sold to them. Most of the Chinese miners worked in organized groups for mutual protection from anti-Chinese violence.

Racial prejudice usually kept them in segregated neighborhoods, but none of the Chinatowns were self-sufficient, so there was interaction with the rest of the population. In Dayton, for example, the Irish-Canadian Walmsley family was friends with and employers of the Chinese. Contrary to popular belief, some stayed in Nevada for the rest of their lives. "Old Jim," one of the original Chinese men in Johnstown, lived there until his death in 1895.

The second major attraction to Nevada was railroad construction. In 1863, plans were laid for the building of the first transcontinental railroad that opened the American West. Charles Crocker, one of the "Big Four" responsible for building the Central Pacific Railroad (CPRR), hired hundreds of Chinese workers, half of whom were already in the United States and the other half through Chinese or Euro American labor contractors in South China. The Chinese workers, who made up about 90 percent of the workforce of 15,000 men, leveled roads, built up roadbeds, cut down trees, built trestles and bridges, created snow sheds, dynamited mountains to create tunnels, and performed hundreds of other tasks as they crossed the Sierra Nevada. In Nevada, they lived in tents and received their pay in a train car that was attached to recreational train cars that provided gambling and women. Chinese workers had to hammer in the final gold and silver spikes at Promontory, Utah, in May 1969 because Leland Stanford of the CPRR and Thomas Durant of the Union Pacific were unable to complete the task. No one knows how many Chinese workers died during construction, but the number was in the thousands. Some Chinese workers went on to build other interstate and intrastate railroad lines, narrow gauges for lumber and mining companies, and roads. Some performed maintenance work, while others opened restaurants, often on land leased from the railroad company, to serve the traveling public. Nevertheless, at the centennial celebration in 1969, the Chinese railroad workers were almost forgotten.

After cutting down trees and clearing roads, some worked in the lumber industry, especially in the Sierra Nevada, and one group even formed its own short-lived lumber and milling company at Glenbrook. Wood was an essential commodity in the building of the West. It has been estimated that 50 to 75 percent of the logging workforce in the Sierra Nevada from about 1870 to the 1910s were Chinese. Newspapers reported as many as 1,000 Chinese people "in the mountains."

Later, mining towns evolved that were scattered throughout Nevada. The Chinese community played an important role in the multi-ethnic mining towns of Tuscarora, Island Mountain, and American Canyon in the 1870 to 1900 era. Some mining crews were multi-racial. There were individual miners as well, but as anti-Chinese movements grew violent, it became more prudent to work in teams of 10 to 20 men. In many of the relatively isolated mining towns, such as Island Mountain, the Chinese often constituted the majority of the population and interethnic harmony among Chinese, Euro Americans, and Native Americans was not uncommon.

The coming of the Chinese coincided with the rise and growth of labor unions and post–Civil War racial anxiety, which led to the spread of anti-Chinese movements and the passage of several anti-Chinese immigration laws put into effect between 1882 and 1924, when the doors were closed to most Chinese immigrants. In the land that welcomed "the poor, tired, and hungry," the Chinese were the first group to be excluded. The 1875 Page Law discouraged Chinese women from immigrating, because they had to prove that they were not prostitutes. The predominately single-men society, although about a third were married with their wives living in China, contributed to the migratory nature of their lifestyle and their indifference to temporary housing. Only diplomats, students, and merchants were among the classes permitted to immigrate.

The men often joined fraternal, district, and family associations as a means of obtaining companionship, protection, mutual aid, funding for major endeavors, and employment assistance. Larger Chinatowns, like Virginia City, had a branch of the Chinese Six Companies (Chinese Consolidated Benevolent Association). Smaller towns had secret brotherhoods like the Chinese Freemasons. These organizations sponsored Chinese New Year's celebrations in many locations, and the Euro American population was often invited to participate.

By the 1870s through the 1950s, Chinese families grew as the second generation of Chinese Americans came of age and started their own families, as seen in Tonopah. The Chinese in Reno popularized traditional Chinese medicine, entertainment, and casinos in the 1920s through the 1950s. The exclusion laws were repealed in 1943 when China and the United States became wartime allies. The repeal allowed 100 Chinese to immigrate annually; most of these were women who started families, gradually balancing the gender ratio by 1980. This created a more stable community.

The civil rights movement of 1954 to 1968 opened new doors of opportunity in all fields, and the Chinese, like other Asians, earned the appellation of "model minority" as they excelled in numerous fields. Chinese American businesses thrived and continued to sponsor traditional festivals. They were no longer segregated into Chinatowns but were free live in other parts of town. They became active in politics and community affairs. The repeal of anti-miscegenation laws allowed greater freedom in selecting marriage partners. The civil rights movement also stimulated an interest in Chinese American history that is now being actively researched and more accurately interpreted.

One
EARLY MINING AND RAILROAD CONSTRUCTION

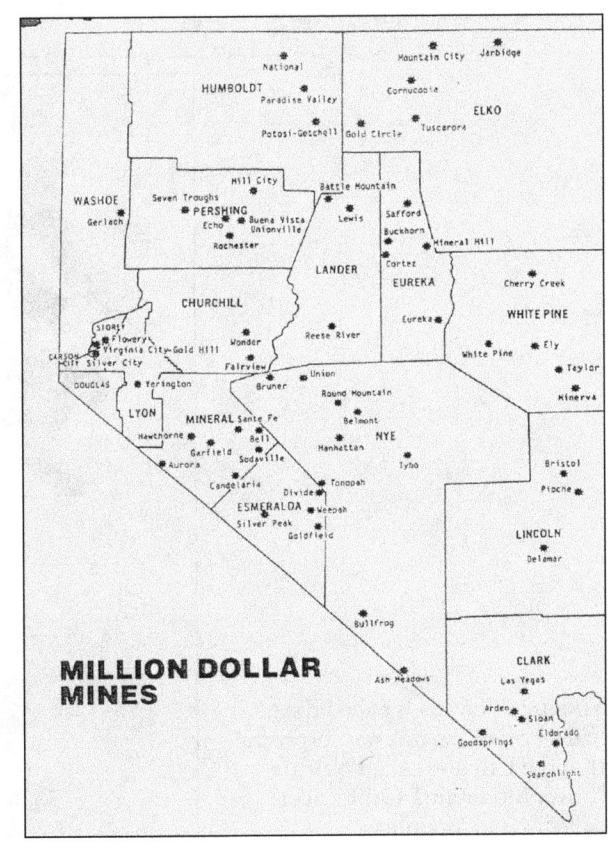

NEVADA MAP. Gold and silver mines were scattered throughout Nevada. Copper, borax, and sulfur mines also employed the Chinese, but it was railroad construction that attracted most Chinese to Nevada in the 1870s. (Dangberg Foundation.)

Year	Total Population in Nevada	Total Chinese Population In U.S.	Chinese Population in Nevada	Percent of Chinese in Nevada	Chinese Males in Nevada	Chinese Females in Nevada	Ratio of Males to Females
1860	6,057	34,933	23	.03	--	--	
1870	42,491	63,199	3,162	7.4	2,817	306	1:9
1880	62,266	105,465	5,416	8.7	5,102	314	1:16
1890	47,355	107,488	2,833	6.0	2,749	84	1:33
1900 Foreign Citizen	42,335	89,863 80,853 9,010	1,352	3.2	1,283	69	1:19
1910 Foreign Citizen	81,875	71,531 56,596 14,935	927	1.1	876	51	1:17
1920 Foreign Citizen	77,407	61,639 43,107 18,532	689	0.9	630	59	1:11
1930 Foreign Citizen	91,058	74,954 44,086 30,868	483	0.5	410	73	1:17
1940 Foreign Citizen	110,247	77,504 37,242 40,262	286	0.3	221	65	1:3
1950 Clark Washoe	160,083	117,629	281 56 82	0.2	205	76	1:3
1960 Clark Washoe	285,278	237,292	572 225 249	0.2	388	184	1:2
1970 Clark Washoe	488,738	433,469	915 457 411	0.2	567	384	1:1.7
1980 Clark Washoe	800,495	812,178	2,979 1,725 1,089	0.4	1,490	1,489	1:1
1990 Foreign Clark Washoe	1,201,833	1,645,472 529,837	6,618 4,185 2,121	0.5	3,180	3,438	1:1
2000 Foreign	1,998,257	2,432,585 988,857	14,113	0.7	N/A	N/A	

POPULATION OF CHINESE IN U.S. AND NEVADA, 1860-2000
Including Foreign-born and Citizens, 1900-1940, 1990-2000
And Clark and Washoe Counties, 1950-1990

POPULATION CHART. The Chinese population in Nevada reached its peak in 1880 at 5,416 (5,102 males, 314 females), or 8.7 percent of the population. The male-to-female ratio did not equalize until 1980. By the early 21st century, the Asian population was the fastest growing minority group in Nevada.

YINSHAN. Nevada is called the "Silver State," so it is not surprising that the Chinese called Nevada "Silver Mountain." California is called "Gold Mountain."

MINER, 1860s. The Chinese miner often carried equipment like the long tom and stoves on a traditional shoulder pole. In 1859, in Gold Canyon, some 50 Chinese gold miners reportedly earned over $35,000. (NHS.)

DAYTON, 2006. This store, one of the few original Chinese buildings in Nevada dating from the mid-1800s, is located in Dayton, one of the two original Chinese settlements.

BIG SAM AND YOO SIN. Yoo Kee (born in 1876), the daughter of Yoo Sin (born in 1850), a cook and one of the four Chinese women living in Dayton in the 1880s, is seen with Big Sam (born in 1822). (NHS.)

MAN, C. 1905. While some men wore traditional Chinese clothing or modifications of the same, others adopted Western-style dress like this man in Dayton. (NHS.)

OSCEOLA DITCH. The Chinese were hired to construct irrigation channels, including the famous Osceola Ditch that cost $250,000 in the 1870s. In May 1877, the largest gold nugget in Nevada, valued at $6,000, was discovered here.

MAN, VIRGINIA CITY, 1880s. This man, probably a merchant, has his tea alongside a narcissus plant, which was introduced from China and blooms during the Chinese New Year. He was a friend of the harness maker, Jacob Kline. (Kline.)

WOMEN. In 1890, the ratio of Chinese women to men was 1 to 33. The 1875 Page Law and 1882 Chinese Exclusion Act made it difficult for women to immigrate. Mary Lock (born in 1842), the wife of Dr. Hop Lock (born in 1815), her son, and her friends are shown at left in this 1860s photograph taken in Virginia City. However, they left around 1871 when Dr. Lock was charged with a crime but found not guilty. Some Chinese women enjoyed the frontier atmosphere of the American West. China Mary, photographed below in 1898, was in this category. She lived in Dutch Flat, California, and Dayton and Virginia City, Nevada. Like many elderly Chinese women living alone, she was fondly remembered for charity work in her later years. She lived to the age of 100. (At left, University of Nevada, Reno Special Collections; below, NHS.)

MRS. G.C. CHAN NEE WONG (DIED IN 1906). Many of the early upper-class Chinese female immigrants had bound feet, a tradition that dated back to the 10th century. She was called Wong (maiden name) Shee (indicating that she was married) by her friends.

OLD HULLY. Old Hully (1830–1916) emigrated in 1870 from Ontario, Canada, and settled in Dayton. He carried produce and other goods on his shoulder pole from Mound House to Virginia City six days a week until he died. (NHS.)

LAUNDRYMAN, C. 1890. Virginia City had 13 Chinese laundrymen in 1860 and 5 in 1870. The laundries were scattered around town. Laundryman Yum Yum (pictured) worked there in the 1890s. (NHS.)

FORMER CHINESE LAUNDRY. Two of the most successful men in Virginia City's Chinatown were laundrymen. From the 1860s to the 1890s, this building located across from the courthouse, photographed here in 2006, was a Chinese laundry.

QUONG KEE (DIED IN 1938). As a cook's apprentice in Virginia City, Quong Kee remarked that the everyday violence was frightening. By 1869, he worked as a cook for the railroad in Elko, specializing in Irish stew. He was present at the Golden Spike Ceremony. When the Central Pacific Railroad met the Union Pacific Railroad in May 1869 at Promontory, Utah, the two last spikes to join the rail lines were one of silver and one of gold. The ceremony marked the completion of the first transcontinental railroad that opened the West and was called the Golden Spike Ceremony. (Arizona Historical Society.)

MANDARIN GARDENS, 2010. Virginia City had at least one Chinese restaurant since the 1860s. The tradition has continued to the present with the Mandarin Garden.

CHINATOWN, C. 1875. This is one of the few photographs of Virginia City's Chinatown. The one-story wooden buildings were typical of the middle-class and lower-middle-class homes of the period. (NHS.)

CHINESE GIANT. Chang Woo Gow (1841–1893) was eight feet tall and weighed 324 pounds. Beginning in 1881, he toured the United States, including Virginia City, with the Barnum and Bailey Circus. (NHS.)

1900. Merchant Ying Yee of Quong Hai Loy filed these partnership papers in 1900 with the Bureau of Immigration, noting that his six partners still lived in Virginia City. (NARA.)

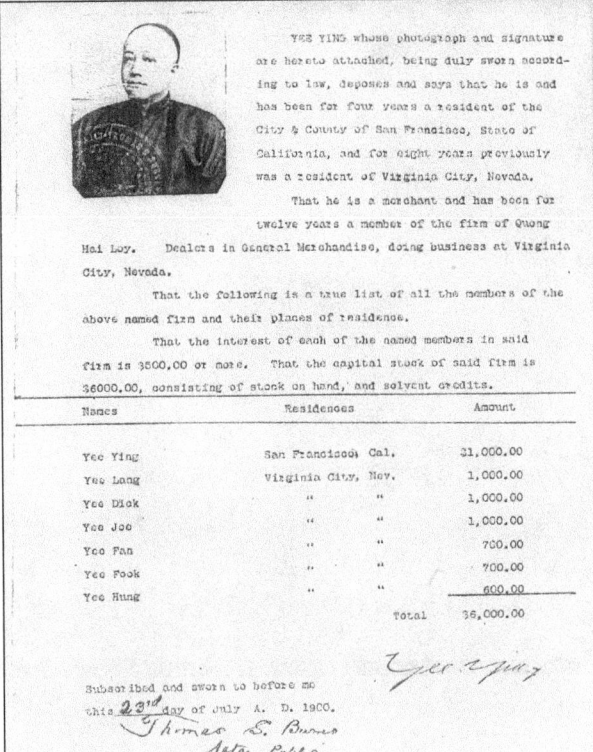

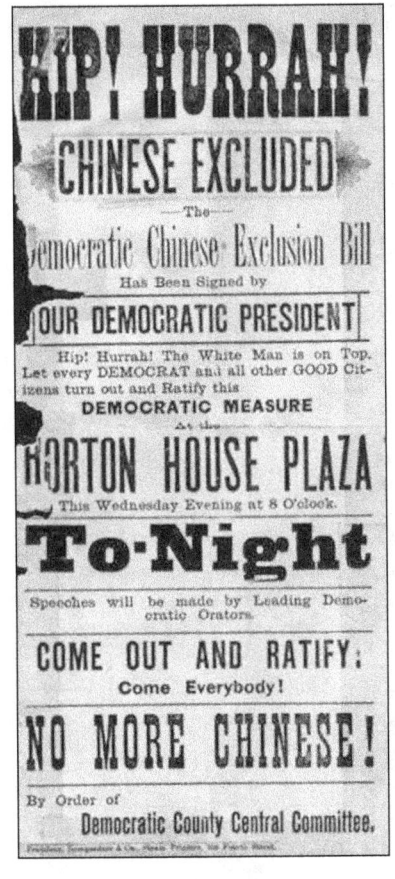

CHINESE EXCLUSION HANDBILL. Anti-Chinese movements became more widespread by the 1870s, which led to the passage of the 1882 Chinese Exclusion Act barring Chinese laborers and women who were not wives of merchants from entering the United States.

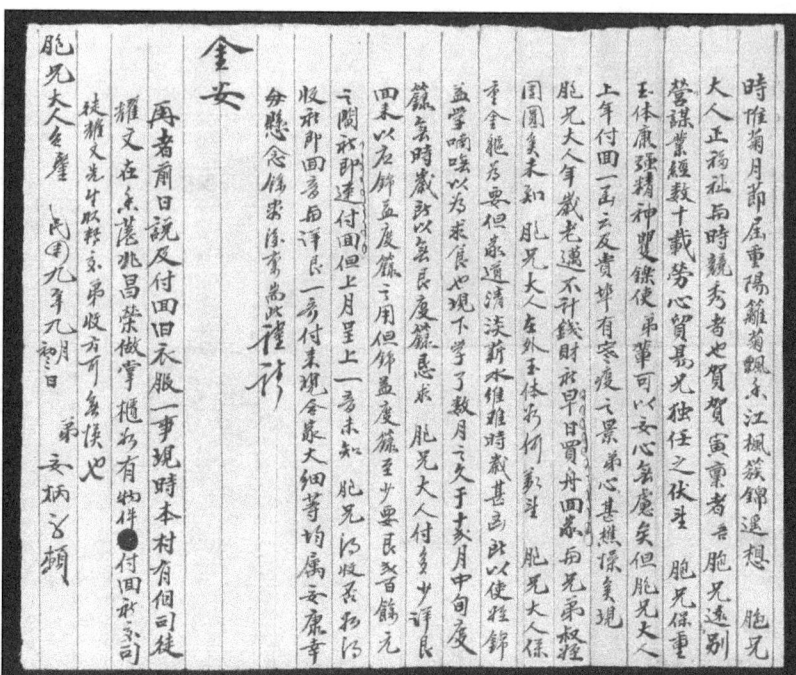

Letter, Dated 1900. Letters to and from home, in this case a younger brother to an older brother, were treasured by the receivers but required a long time in transit and the ability to read and write Chinese. (NSM.)

Cortez. Chinese cooks learned to prepare American meals, including W. Gen (born in 1842), who worked as a cook in 1870 and lived with the teamster C. Jones (born in 1841) in Cortez, a mining town that was founded in 1862. (NENM.)

BUILDING THE CENTRAL PACIFIC AND OTHER LINES. The Chinese built some fantastic bridges for the Central Pacific Railroad. The one seen above across the Truckee River near Reno, constructed in the 1870s, is an example of the engineering feat that they accomplished. Beginning in 1863, the Chinese worked on the construction of railroad lines, including the Central Pacific Railroad and local/regional lines. They cut down trees, leveled roads, and built tunnels, bridges, snow sheds, roundhouses, and stations, often working in teams of 50 to 75. Later, they maintained the roads, tracks, and trains. Some were housed in white tents along the construction route, as seen in the 1868 photograph below at Brown's Station near Winnemucca. (Above, NSRM; below, NHS.)

RAILROAD TRAIN AND TENT HOUSING. Whenever possible, a supply train, often with James Strobridge's private car, was near the tent housing. The Chinese headman distributed the salary and supplied the Chinese with food, including chicken and rice, and tea for a charge. (NSM.)

CHINESE TRACK-LAYING CREW. Based on their work on the Central Pacific, the Chinese laid tracks for other local and regional lines, as seen in the crew at Empire near Carson City, Nevada, laying tracks for the Virginia and Truckee Railroad. (NSM.)

COMPLETING THE TRANSCONTINENTAL RAILROAD. When the construction workers reached present-day Reno, only about 5,000 men were retained to finish the work across Nevada. With a crew of 4,000 men, mostly Chinese and some Irish, the Central Pacific Railroad team laid 10 miles and 65 feet of track in 12 hours. The record has not been matched despite modern equipment. The Union Pacific and Central Pacific were joined on May 10, 1869, at Promontory, Utah. Below, at least one Chinese worker in a hat with his back to the cameraman is visible in Andrew J. Russell's "East Meets West" photograph. Reno was originally called Lake's Crossing, and only after the railroad was completed was the name changed to Reno. (Below, Oakland Museum.)

JUPITER ENGINE. This recently restored engine was a 4-4-0 steam locomotive that made history when it met with the Union Pacific's No. 119 to connect the first transcontinental railroad line on May 10, 1869.

FEATHER RIVER CANYON WPRR, 1907. After May 1869, the Chinese worked on other interstate and intrastate lines, including the Western Pacific Railroad along the Feather River Canyon in California near Nevada. (NHS.)

COMMEMORATION. With inscriptions in English and Chinese, the memorial seen at right in Sparks, originally a railroad town located near Reno, honored the Chinese railroad workers, and a small section of the original railroad track was placed in the nearby park. Ignored by the Railroad Centennial Committee, the Chinese community, led by the Chinese Historical Society of America, established its own bronze plaque, seen below, to commemorate the Chinese workers at Promontory, Utah, in May 1969. They refused to allow the 15,000 or more Chinese workers laboring for the Central Pacific Railroad to be forgotten.

TO COMMEMORATE THE CENTENNIAL OF THE FIRST TRANSCONTINENTAL RAILROAD IN AMERICA AND TO PAY TRIBUTE TO THE CHINESE WORKERS OF THE CENTRAL PACIFIC RAILROAD WHOSE INDOMITABLE COURAGE MADE IT POSSIBLE.

MAY 10, 1869 – MAY 10, 1969
PLAQUE PLACED BY
THE CHINESE HISTORICAL SOCIETY OF AMERICA
PLAQUE DONATED BY
SAN FRANCISCO CHINESE COMMUNITY

GEE, CHEF AT DEPOT HOTEL, ELKO, C. 1892. Crews and passengers needed food, and the railroad companies sometimes supplemented the income of Chinese restaurant owners to keep their restaurants along the rail lines open 24 hours a day. (NHS.)

CARSON CITY'S CHINATOWN, 1930s. Carson City had a Chinatown about five blocks long. In 1935, a fire destroyed many of the commercial buildings, and by 1937 only 13 Chinese residents lived in the city. (NHS.)

CHINESE SIX COMPANIES, C. 1907 AND FREEMASONS, C. 1939. In 1907, a man stands in front of Carson City's Chinese Six Companies Association, which acted as the primary intermediary between the Chinese and Euro American communities. It represented the Chinese district organizations, so membership was based upon birthplace. The Chinese Freemasons, or Zhigongtang, a secret fraternal society with elected membership and the second most powerful organization, had sufficient funds to build a two-story local branch based upon a predetermined design. Both organizations established their national headquarters in San Francisco and had branches in Carson City. (NHS.)

KENO. Among the many games of chance that the Chinese introduced to Nevada was keno, which was based upon an 80-character poem from the Confucian *Thousand Character Book* that is read by elementary schoolchildren. It begins, "[The colors of] Heaven and Earth are black and yellow." In 1889, the Carson City *Morning Appeal* described the game and publicized the winnings of one local Euro American resident who bet 55¢ and won $900 at the local Chinese laundry. Eventually, the Chinese version was converted to 80 numbers and moved from being played in Chinese laundries to casinos and gaming establishments.

CARSON CITY'S CHINATOWN, 1935, AND MRS. SAMUEL GIBSON. Samuel Gibson (Non Chong Yee) was the leader of Carson City's Chinatown, a labor contractor for lumbering and railroad companies, and manager of the prosperous Quong Hing (later Nom Wah) General Store. He owned one entire block in Chinatown, and his wife operated two boardinghouses for workers in the area. Their two daughters and one son were born and raised in Carson City until the anti-Chinese violence of 1866–1867 broke out. The Gibsons took two of the children back to China, where they remained for the rest of their lives, and left Ah Cum, the elder daughter, with friends in nearby Benton. (Above, Stoldal; at right, Kee.)

AH CUM KEE AND BROTHER KING YEE. When her parents returned to China, Ah Cum went to live with her adopted parents, married Chung Kee, and began a family of six children. Ah Cum Kee (1876–1929) is pictured above with her two children and her adopted parents in traditional Chinese clothing. Her brother King Yee, at left, returned to Carson City in 1900 to work at Quong Hing. His father's good friend, the wealthy and influential Duane L. Bliss, testified on his behalf for his reentry. King Yee had difficulty adjusting to American culture. He later worked at a Quong Hing store in Texas, where he died. (Above, Kee; at left, NARA.)

HOMES IN CHINATOWN. This residential area shows the simple one-story wooden construction that was typical of many Chinese homes in Chinatown throughout the American West. Above, a man sits outside his Carson City home, and a chicken, which undoubtedly provided fresh eggs, walks on the wooden sidewalk in the 1930s. The homes declined by 1935 as the Depression led to the abandonment of much of Carson City's Chinatown. In the 1870s, the stream in front of the houses had a waterwheel that served as an inspiration for the later Ferris wheel. (Above, NHS; below, Stoldal.)

CHINESE DAOIST FORTUNE-TELLER. An 1870s or 1880s poster of a traveling Daoist priest and fortune teller indicated that he provided information on feng shui (geomancy), health, and other matters and represented one of major Daoist sects from China. He wears a Western-style hat and boots but Chinese top and pants. Daoist and Buddhist priests were reclassified as "laborers" in the 1892 extension of the 1882 Chinese Exclusion Act and, therefore, could no longer immigrate freely to the United States. This left Chinese immigrants without traditional spiritual leaders. As a result, many Chinese turned to Christianity by the 1920s. (NSM.)

Two

Logging and Later Mining Towns

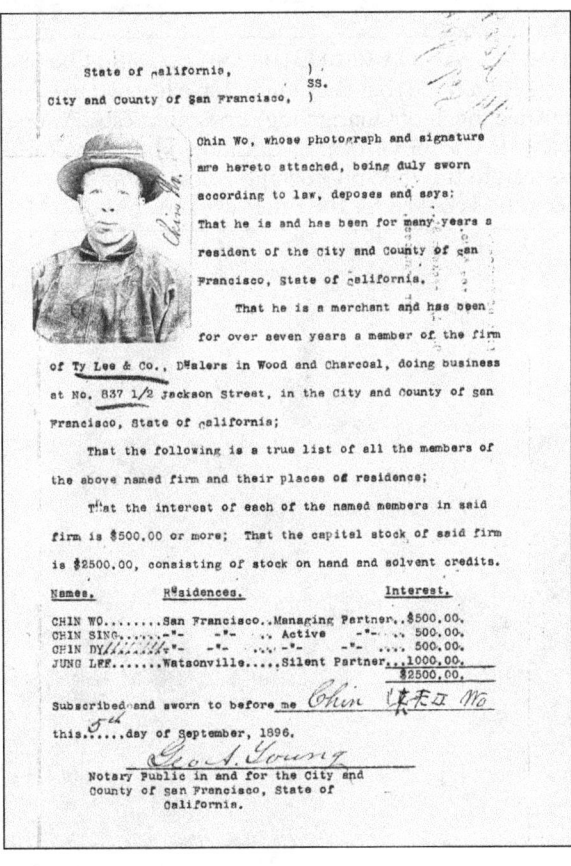

CHIN WO, 1896. Approximately 70 percent of the woodcutters in the Sierra Nevada in the 1870s were Chinese. They sold their cut logs to Virginia City, Reno, and San Francisco. San Francisco wood dealer Chin Wo was probably one of the recipients of the wood. Chinese woodcutters worked from the 1870s to 1910s in the mountains surrounding Lake Tahoe.

JAMES CANYON LUMBER CAMP AND LOGGING OXENS. The Chinese performed a variety of tasks in logging, a trade that they might have learned in China but lost because the Manchu government burned much of Guangdong's coastal forests. At one time, they had their own lumber company based in Glenbrook near Lake Tahoe. The Chinese often loaded and unloaded the wood on flatcars, as seen in the 1868 photograph below, trimmed the trees, and cut the lumber into specified sizes, as well as cooked for the other workers. (Above, NHS; below, NSM.)

FLUME AND LUMBER YARD. The Chinese worked as flume tenders to keep the logs moving long distances, as seen in the photograph at left of the Clear Creek Flume. In 2002, the US Forest Service sponsored an archaeological excavation of a Chinese cabin near this flume in Spooner Summit. The flume ended in Carson City (now the site of the Nevada State Railroad Museum), where the Carson Tahoe Lumber and Fluming Company cut the logs into boards and shipped them to Virginia City, Reno, and elsewhere via the Virginia and Truckee Railroad and its connection to the Transcontinental Railroad (also called the Central Pacific). (At right, NHS; below, NSRM.)

LOGGING TRAIN AND VERDI BOX FACTORY, 1888. The Chinese often loaded and unloaded the lumber onto the trains. They worked in several different kinds of related factories, including Oliver Lonkey's prosperous box factory in Verdi that employed 45 men, including many Chinese, and had the usual relatively self-sufficient lumber camp. At this time, Verdi was considered a lumberman's paradise, but by the early 1900s clear cutting, fires, and insect invasions diminished the forest. In 2003, a forest service–sponsored archaeological excavation of a Chinese site took place in the vicinity of the box factory. (Below, NHS.)

DESTRUCTION OF FORESTS. The demand for lumber was so great, especially on the Comstock during the boom years when the Virginia and Truckee made 44 daily trips with lumber, that the landscape of the Sierra Nevada was denuded of trees. The situation was compounded by forest fires and infestations, as well as other problems created by man and nature. (NSRM.)

TUSCARORA MINERS. Between the 1870s and 1890s, there were several multi-ethnic mining crews in Tuscarora, one of the most profitable mining sites in Nevada during that era. (NENM.)

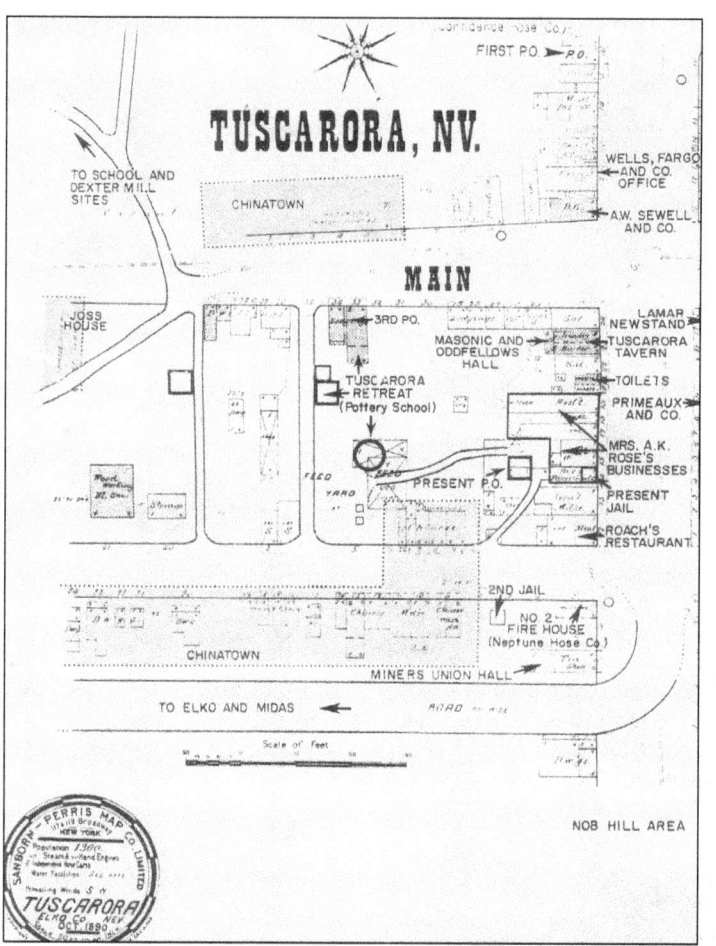

TUSCARORA. In the 1870 census, Tuscarora counted 104 Chinese and 15 Euro Americans. But the town quickly grew, and as many as 2,000 Chinese were said to live there in the 1880s. At first, the Chinese settled in Old Tuscarora, and the Hop Sing Tong dominated the community. Later, New Tuscarora, shown near bottom of the 1890 Sanborn-Perris map, was built, and the Chinese Freemasons established their two-story lodge on Main Street, seen in the lower right of photograph below. The town experienced economic decline in the early 1900s. By 1920, the population of the town was 50, which included five Chinese (two miners, a ranch hand, a restaurateur, and laundry man). Today, it is regarded as a ghost town with fewer than 50 residents. (At left, Sanborn map; below, NENM.)

ALTAR. The Chinese Freemasons' intricately carved gilded altar in Tuscarora honoring Guan Yu, the deity of literature, loyalty, and war, was located on the second floor of the lodge building. It was eventually relocated to Frontier Village in Las Vegas in the 1950s but has since disappeared. Parts of the altar decorations are in the Nevada State Museum, Las Vegas. The altar in the Bok Kai Temple in Marysville, California, illustrates how it might have looked. Both altars were built in the 1880s. (At right, NSM LV.)

AH LEE LAKE AND CHINESE ROBE. Ah Lee Lake (born in 1855 and immigrated in 1869) was the leader of the Chinese Freemasons, a labor contractor, and the owner of a general merchandising store in Tuscarora. He is photographed at left in a fur-lined silk jacket not unlike the fur-lined silk Chinese robe from the Walter Tun family of Reno, now in the textile collection at Nevada State Museum, Carson City. Ah Lee Lake, who knew English and Chinese, served as the intermediary between the Chinese and Euro American communities. He was a good friend of the French-Canadian Primeaux family. (At left, NENM; below, NSM.)

AH LEE LAKE (RIGHT) AND CHIN FOOK (BELOW). These men were two of the eight partners of Tuscarora's prosperous Quong Hing Lung and Company that catered to Chinese and non-Chinese alike in one of Nevada's rich gold mining towns of the 1870s to early 1900s. Due to immigration regulations, they had to file partnership papers with the American government in the 1890s. Ah Lee Lake, one of the wealthiest Chinese men in Elko County, was well liked by the Euro American community. The local newspaper reported that he even traveled by train to New York around 1920. (NARA.)

ISLAND MOUNTAIN. Located near Tuscarora was the small mining community of Island Mountain, established in 1873 and abandoned by the 1920s. The Chinese constituted the majority of the population, and some friendships were long lasting among the Chinese, Euro Americans, and Shoshones. During the 1870s to 1890s, it was a major stagecoach stop between the transcontinental railroad stations at Elko or Carlin and the stations in southern Idaho. Hilda Matthey, whose husband was a mine investor, photographed Island Mountains's two main roads, Peking and Hangchow Streets, and the teamsters bringing a load of goods to the main store owned and operated by China Lem in 1903. In 2007, Vegas PBS produced a film called *Island Mountain Days: Discovering Nevada's Chinese Miners*, detailing its history.

ISLAND MOUNTAIN AND CHINA LEM. In 1903, Dr. Heinrich Matthey and his wife, Hilda, visited the mine that they had invested in. Hilda, a professional photographer, took pictures of the community of Island Mountain. Seen above, China Lem (born 1833, Chinese name Hong Lem Ng) opened his general merchandising store around 1873, sold Western and Asian goods, and was the community leader. Initially, his store was built with local materials and featured wooden barrels with river sand for preserving fresh cabbage, carrots, onions, and other produce for winter use. Later, he built his store out of lumber. Fishermen, hunters, and tourists liked to gather at Lem's. Euro Americans included him in dinner invitations at their homes and cared for him when he was ill. Lem was one of the wealthiest Chinese residents of Elko County.

ADVERTISEMENT. Like many Chinese merchants of this era, China Lem advertised his store in the local newspaper in order to attract Euro American customers, as seen in the lower right-hand corner of the photograph.

EXCAVATION. From 1999 until 2001, the forest service's Passport in Time program recruited volunteers, including many from the Wing Luke Museum in Seattle. Middle school student Alexander Solomon wrote about his experience at www.passportintime.com/summaries/99/nv99a_islandmt.html.

ARTIFACTS. The archaeological excavation, supervised by University of Nevada, Reno graduate students working under Prof. Donald Hardesty during 1999 to 2001, yielded many items. There were shards of pottery, bottles, jars, a rusted Log Cabin maple syrup tin, gaming pieces, Chinese medicine bottles, buttons, nails, a coffee machine, an abacus, and fragments of pages of a Chinese book that discussed the new 1912 Republican government in China. The book and abacus probably belonged to the merchant China Lem. Found all over the 14 structures were Chinese stomach medicine bottles, indicating a common health problem. Patricia Hunt-Jones of the University of Nevada, Reno wrote her master's thesis about this site.

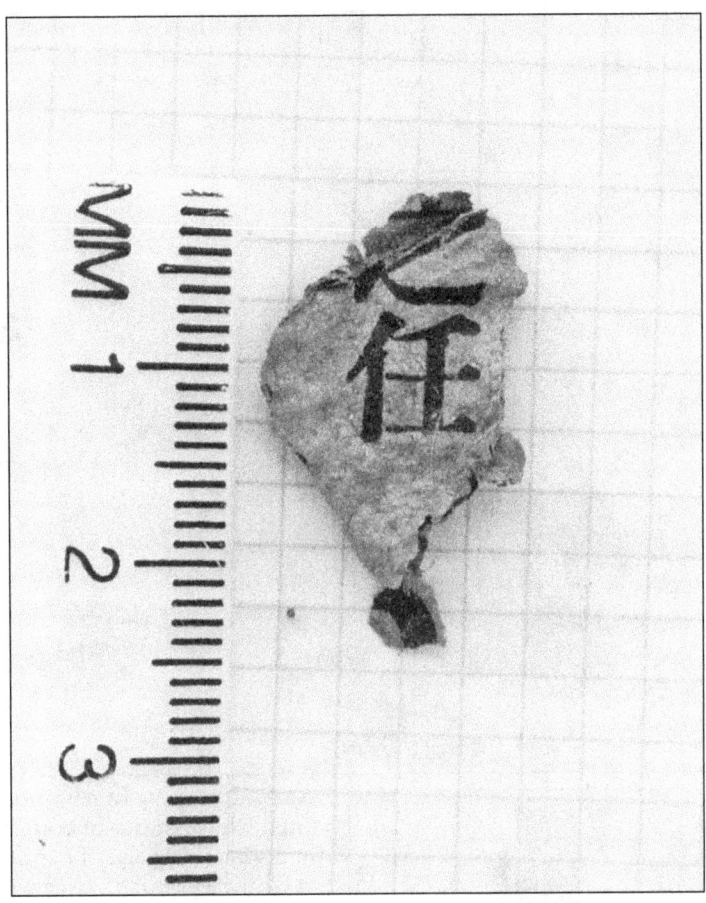

ARTIFACTS FROM ELSEWHERE. Chinese archaeological sites usually have shards of pottery and containers refashioned into something else. They often contained empty bottles of Chinese *ng gai pei* (rice wine). Rice wine was used for drinking, medicinal soups, and for rubbing on injuries. The front and back of one type of rice wine bottle is shown above. China Lem's store had an unusually high-quality wine bottle that was iridescent blue (not shown). Pictured to the left is an opium lamp made from a soda bottle manufactured in Eureka, Nevada. China Lem opposed opium smoking, so there was little opium-smoking paraphernalia in Island Mountain. (At left, AACC.)

Henly. Henly (born in 1843, married in 1871, and immigrated in 1881) was a placer miner who acted as a guide for Dr. and Hilda Matthey of Iowa when they visited Island Mountain in 1903. Hilda, a professional photographer, snapped a shot of Henly behind a piece of Joshua Hendy mining equipment that was manufactured in San Francisco. Much of the equipment used in Island Mountain was purchased from San Francisco. Matthey also photographed Henly's home, located down the road from Chinatown. The house is more elaborate than the other homes in Island Mountain. His spaniel is visible in the front of the house.

HOMES AND RESERVOIR. The homes on Hangchow Street in Island Mountain were small and built into the hillside to maintain heat in the winter and create a cooling effect in the summer. Originally, a small reservoir was constructed to provide water for placer mining, but in 1897 a project to enlarge the reservoir was launched, and some 200 workers, mostly Chinese, were hired to do the construction work. Euro Americans were paid at the same rate as the Chinese workers for the same jobs, but supervisors, who were only Euro Americans, were paid more. By 1900, despite this effort to revitalize mining, the industry had declined and most of the miners left. A few Chinese miners, however, remained until the 1910s.

HARDMAN HOTEL, 1926. One of the few structures remaining in nearby Gold Creek was the Hardman Hotel, whose Chinese cook stands with members of the US Forest Service in this 1920s image. By 1930, Gold Creek was abandoned. (Forest Service.)

HEADSTONES. China Lem's closest friends were the Nep brothers, placer miners and ranchers. Suey Nep died in 1898 (incorrectly listed as 1897), and his brother Joe died in 1915. (Forest Service.)

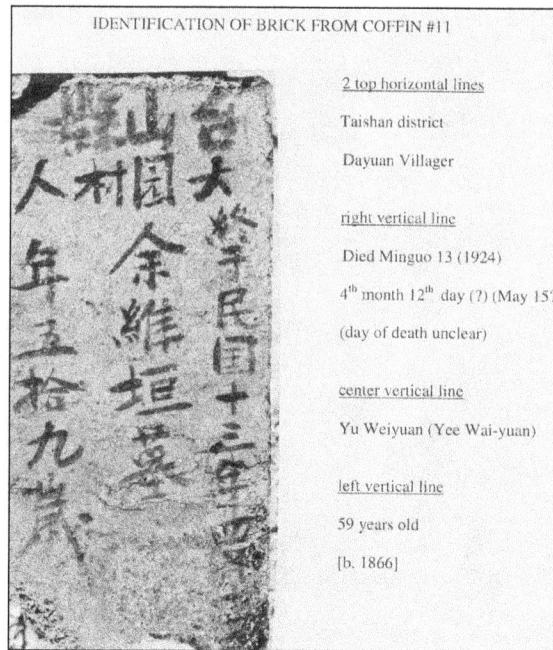

IDENTIFICATION OF BRICK FROM COFFIN #11

<u>2 top horizontal lines</u>
Taishan district
Dayuan Villager

<u>right vertical line</u>
Died Minguo 13 (1924)
4th month 12th day (?) (May 15?)
(day of death unclear)

<u>center vertical line</u>
Yu Weiyuan (Yee Wai-yuan)

<u>left vertical line</u>
59 years old
[b. 1866]

HEADSTONE AND BONE CONTAINERS. Traditionally, a Chinese headstone stated the name, birthplace, birth date, death date, and, sometimes, age of the person, as seen in this example from the Carlin Chinese Cemetery. Most Chinese were buried in cemeteries owned by their associations, and if they had death insurance, their bodies were professionally exhumed after six or seven years and the bones scrapped and cleaned before being placed in ceramic or metal containers for reburial in their home villages in China. Unfortunately, the Sino-Japanese War of 1931 to 1945 interrupted the usual shipment of bones to China, so many had their final resting place in the American West. Elko County was home to a Chinese "bone house" in its Chinese section of the public cemetery, but by the middle of the 20th century it was empty.

Three

INTO THE 20TH CENTURY

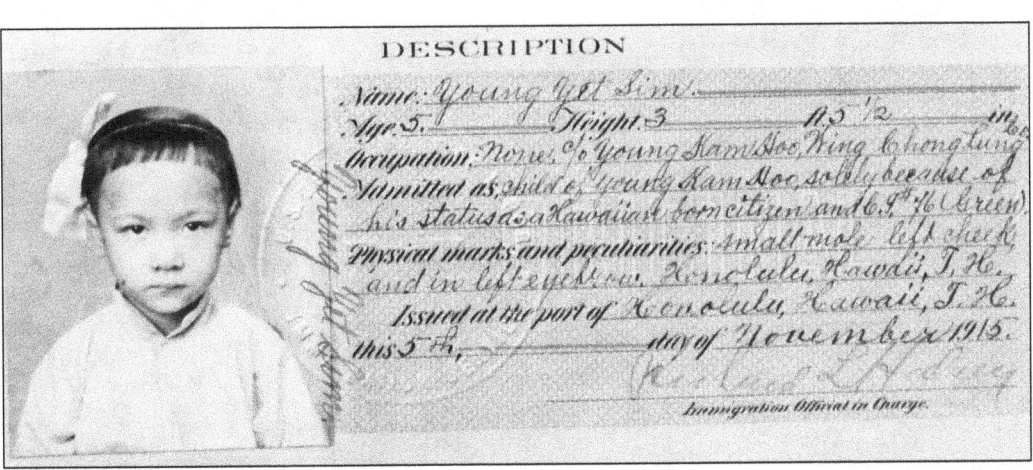

CERTIFICATE OF IDENTITY. In 1892, a new federal law required all Chinese to have a certificate of identity and/or a certificate of residence, regardless of whether he or she was born in China or the United States.

CERTIFICATE OF RESIDENCE. Most Chinese had certificates of residence. The Chinese Six Companies regarded this practice as illegal and discriminatory and advised their members not to comply. The Chinese Freemasons decided that they had no option and advised their members to obey. An 1893 court ruling forced all Chinese residents to obtain the required documentation, and if the certificate was destroyed or lost, a duplicate had to be in the person's possession. Otherwise, the person was subject to immediate arrest and possible deportation. The harsh practice ended in 1920. (NARA.)

APPLICATION. In 1908, Yim Chew lost his certificate of residence and applied for a duplicate copy. Thousands of Chinese did the same thing, and these records are on file at the National Archives and Records Administration in Washington, DC. In 1911, the Immigration Service sent Yim Chew the analysis of the situation in a three-page letter (only two pages shown) that decided Euro Americans had stolen his original certificate and it was not lost in a fire as he claimed. Nevertheless, the Bureau of Immigration issued him a duplicate certificate that allowed him to remain in the United States. Sometimes, the bureau was not as forgiving. (NARA.)

Department of Commerce and Labor
IMMIGRATION SERVICE

OFFICE OF THE COMMISSIONER
SAN FRANCISCO, CAL.

Sadramento, Calif.,
Aug. 21, 1911.

Chinese Inspector in Charge,
    Angel Island, Cal.

Sir:

    In re YIM CHEW, applicant for duplicate certificate of residence, Ser. No. 196:

    This applicant is 57 or 58 years of age; claims to have forgotten his date of birth as he came when very young; been in the United States over forty years; is now a merchant,- manager of Kwong Chung Co., 102 N. Center Street, Reno, Nev.; claims to have been registered at Independence, Cal., he at that time living at Big Pine; that all the Chinese living in the vicinity of Big Pine and Bishop were called to Independence where they were registered; remembers the names of two who were registered at the same time, Mow Wo Sang and Lee Duck; thinks he was registered as a merchant as at that time he was selling clothes throughout the country; that after registration he remained in California six or seven months and went from there to Carson, Nev., and after remaining there six or seven months he went to Reno where he has been ever since; claims to have lost his certificate K.S. 34-10-4 (Oct. 27, 1908)

    The cause of the fire or fires in Chinatown on that date was that the people that owned the grounds on which China-

2
Yim Chew.

town was located had been trying for a long time to get them to vacate so that they could rent the premises to women of the halfworld; these Chinamen having ground leases refused to vacate and as I understand it their shacks were condemned by the health officer as being unsanitary. After this condemnation a lot of men went into Chinatown and pulled down quite a number of houses after which they burned the lumber. This applicant had to leave his house in a hurry and did not have a chance to move all of his effects, but he was helped by a few white men to get some things out of the house, and he claims to have lost his certificate at that time. In my opinion this man's certificate was not burned but some of the people in helping him move his effects saw the envelope with his bank stock and his certificate and they simply took it. My reasons for making this assertion are that there was a fire in Reno Chinatown several years ago in one of the Chinese stores at which time almost everything was taken from the burning building, and after being removed more than two-thirds of it was stolen by white people; at least that is the claim made by the Chinese.

    This applicant has absolutely no proof that he lost his certificate at the time and in the manner stated, but he has lived in Reno for the past fifteen or sixteen years; is known to almost every business man in the city and bears an excellent reputation. The affidavits of Mr. Stanaway and Mr.

34. Joss House, Chinatown, Winnemucca, Nev.

WINNEMUCCA. Winnemucca's original Chinatown was built on land leased from the Central Pacific Railroad (CPRR). Many of the original Chinese residents were railroad workers. When the Chinese became more prosperous, they decided to move to Baud Street on the outskirts of town and away from the railroad tracks. The new Chinatown was built according to feng shui (geomancy), so the structures did not follow the lot lines. The "joss house," so named for the joss sticks used in religious ceremonies, was actually a Chinese Freemason lodge in the center of the new Chinatown. By the 1930s, it had become a community center. (Stodal.)

WINNEMUCCA'S CHINATOWN. Volunteers for the Nevada State Museum constructed a diorama (below) of what Chinatown in Winnemucca looked like in 1910 based upon the drawings of Thomas Chew, who grew up there and wrote a detailed description of the buildings, garden, and activities as he knew it. Quong On Long was one of the major general stores and was owned by Hee Sing Low (1851–1921), a supporter of the 1911 Revolution led by Sun Yatsen. Although some of the land is still vacant today, the Masonic lodge and public library on Baud Street now mark the location of Winnemucca's second Chinatown. (NSM.)

SUN YATSEN. Sun Yatsen (1866-1925, seen at left), born in Zhongshan, Guangdong, was educated in Hawaii. He led a revolutionary movement to overthrow the Manchu rulers of China and gained support from the overseas Chinese, especially those in the United States. On one of his successful fundraising trips, he stopped in Reno and Winnemucca. In Winnemucca, one of the community leaders, Wing Low (seen in the upper left-hand corner of the photograph below), presented Sun with a check for $3,500 for the revolutionary cause. On October 10, 1911, the Republic of China was established with Sun Yatsen as the first provisional president. (At left, NARA; below, Him Mark Lai.)

AMERICAN CANYON. Located near Winnemucca was the mining community of American Canyon. Placer gold mining was at its height between 1881 and 1895. Wong Kee was one of the most prominent mine owners and employed 900 men to work for him in placer and hard rock mining. In a 1913 interview, the Chinese caretaker of the local Chinese Freemason lodge told a reporter that the Chinese had removed $20 million from the site. Wong Kee had loaned Walter E. Scott (1872–1954), also known as "Death Valley Scotty," money. When the two men met in Rhyolite in 1907, the local restaurants would not serve Wong Kee because he was Chinese, so Scott purchased lunch, and in protest the men sat in the middle of the main street with Scott's trusty rifle at his side. (NHS.)

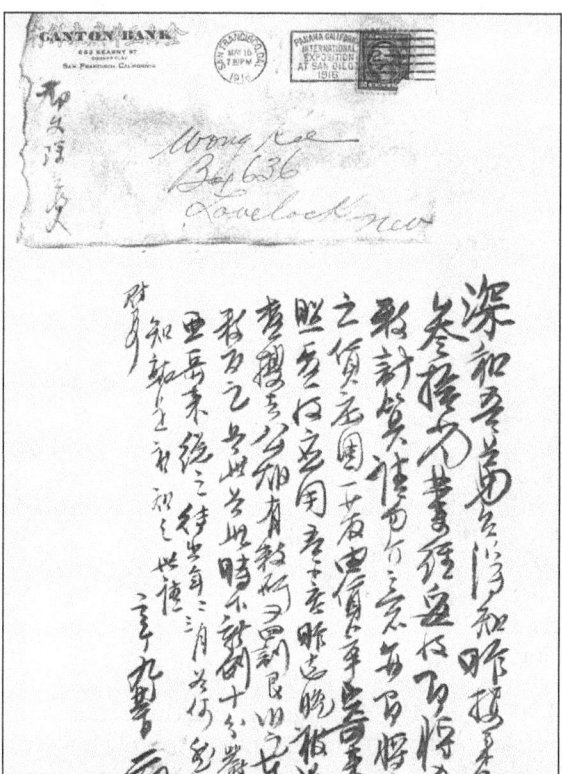

BANK OF CANTON. The Bank of Canton in San Francisco handled the transfer of money for many miners, including Wong Kee, as seen in this letter in Chinese sent to his home in Lovelock. (NSM.)

CHINA CAMP. Many Chinese mining camps were abandoned. In 1970, Robert Morrill visited China Camp on the border of California and Nevada and took this photograph of remains of one of the Chinese cabins. (Morrill.)

ELY, C. 1905. In 1870, there were 292 Chinese in White Pine County, and in 1890 the figure dropped to 46. A Chinatown was built in Ely in a segregated neighborhood off the main highway. (NHS.)

CHINESE COWBOY. Some Chinese worked as cowboys in Nevada. In 1913, the man dressed in white chaps seen here won the rodeo in Elko. He reportedly had training in the martial arts. (NHS.)

CARSON CITY. Ormsby County Assessment of Property in 1870 demonstrated the wealth of Carson City's Dr. Ah Kee as his possessions, including several improved lots, merchandise in his general store, a wagon, two horses, and a gold watch, are listed. In 1877, he influenced the superintendent of schools to allow his children (and all Chinese children in Nevada) to attend public school. Yee Bong, who was born in Virginia City around 1877, eventually settled in Carson City, where he began as a cook in a hotel and then opened his own popular café in the heart of Chinatown. In the 1930s, he was one of oldest Chinese residents and, a decade later, one of the last. (Below, Stoldal.)

Four

Second Generation Chinese and Their Families

Chinese Wedding Dress. Despite the highly uneven ratio of women to men (one to 19 in 1900, one to 17 in 1910, one to 11 in 1920, and one to 17 in 1930), some men found wives, married, and had children in the early 20th century. These families had more opportunities than their ancestors, and many had adopted American customs and values. (NSM.)

HAWTHORNE. Many Chinese came from Kaiping, Guangdong, and sent money home to build new Western-style houses like the one seen to the left. Chung Kee (1847–1909), a gardener, vegetable peddler, and general merchandising store owner, came from Kaiping. The name of his store, Chung Kee, gave him his "American" name. He taught the nearby Paiutes on the Walker River/Schurz Reservation how to dry farm. His white, stringless celery and other produce graced the tables of elegant urban hotels in San Francisco and Salt Lake City. Like many leaders of the Chinese community, he paid taxes on behalf of many of the Chinese in Hawthorne, translated documents, and assisted them in legal and other matters. He married Carson City–born Ah Cum in 1890. He was buried in 1909 in the Hawthorne Chinese Cemetery. (At left, Landon Quan; below, Kee.)

AH CUM KEE. In 1890, Ah Cum (1876–1929) married Chung Kee and raised their six children in Hawthorne, Tonopah, Virginia City, and Reno. In the 1907 photograph at right, she is with her children Charles (1893–1977), May (1895–1965), Florence (1897–1919), Myrtle (1901–986), William (1903–1956), and Frank (1906–1989), along with their two dogs. When her husband died in 1909, she took over the farm and became the first Chinese American female farmer in Nevada. However, times were difficult, so she moved to Tonopah, where the photograph below was taken, because her close friends, including the Fords, lived there. Her public school education in Carson City and Benton gave her fluency in English, and news reporters enjoyed interviewing her. She made the transition to Western dress because her son Charles had been teased at school for wearing Chinese clothing. She was very liberal in her outlook. (Kee.)

LOY FORD. In 1899, Loy Lee (1882–1921), born in Sacramento, married William Min Chung Ford (1850–1922), a Chinese borax-mining boss and labor contractor in Candelaria who was given his American name by close friends. They wore traditional Chinese clothing for the ceremony, and the entire town attended the celebration. Ah Cum and her two oldest children also attended the wedding. In December 1899, Loy gave birth to Timothy Tianbon Ford. Ford insisted on giving his children American names, often selecting names of friends or famous historic people. (Lym.)

FORDS IN TONOPAH. In 1900, James Butler founded "the second Comstock" (anticipated as a rich source of mineral wealth) and the town, originally a tent city, was later named Tonopah. The Fords relocated there as one of the first families and built a one-story home on the outskirts of Chinatown. Below, Loy Ford stands in a Chinese outfit with her two boys, Timothy (left) and James Butler Ford (1902–1955), on their front porch in 1903. Later, she adopted American-style clothing and ways. Her husband was described in the local newspaper as "the most Americanized Chinese" in the mining town. (Above, NSM; below, CNHS.)

ANTI-CHINESE RIOT. Because the railroad was going to connect Tonopah to other major cities, many union workers in Tonopah were afraid that the Chinese population would grow. On September 3, 1903, a mob led by union officers rushed into Chinatown to drive the Chinese out. They left Loy Ford and her children alone because they knew that her husband was influential in the community. However, they severely beat and then dragged old Chong Bing Long (1837–1903, also known as Sing Lee), owner of the Sing Lee Laundry across the street from the Union Hall, out into the desert where he died from his wounds. His body was found the next day. Some of the union men went on trial in Belmont but were found innocent because the testimonies of Chinese eyewitnesses were deemed inadmissible in a Christian court of law. (CNHS.)

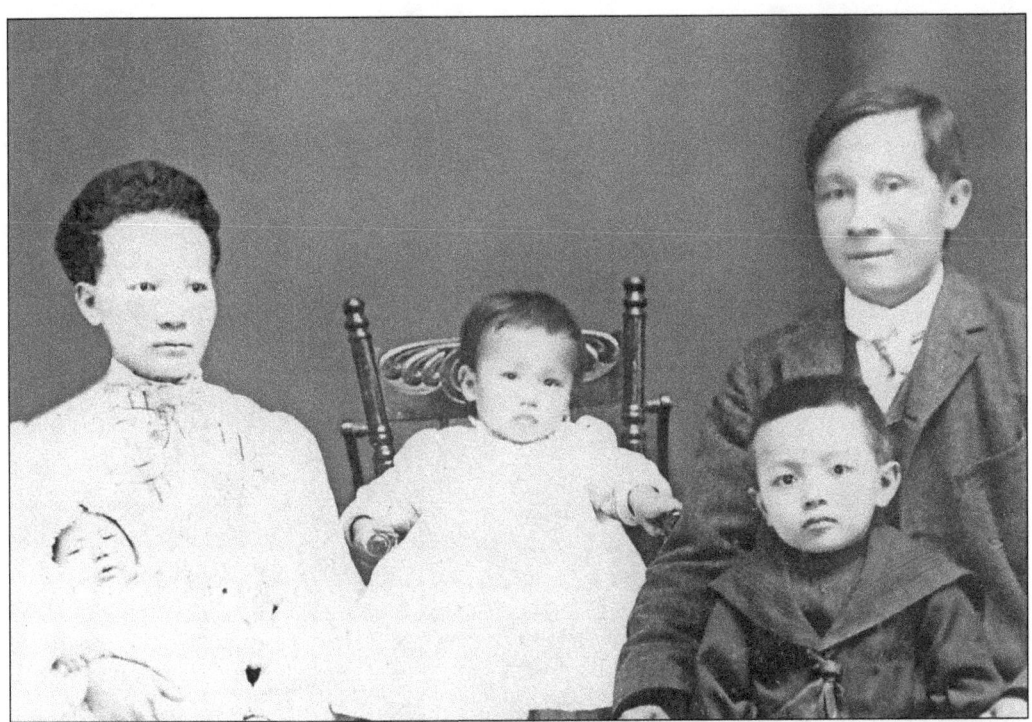

FORD FAMILY. In 1905, Loy Ford gave birth to Rose (1905–1973), and the family had a photograph taken of the new baby, James (center), Timothy, and father William. Because she and the boys had taken refuge during the 1903 riot in the home of a Euro American family, she learned American customs and was given the name Lilly (because she was "like a flower"). By this time, Loy wore American clothing. William also opened the Barnum boarding house with his partner, Charles Chung (1850–1914), located across the street from the newspaper office. The attached restaurant fed many of the townspeople. Their attorney was Key Pittman (1872–1940), Nevada's US senator from 1913 to 1940. Another close friend was Nevada power broker George Wingfield (1876–1959). James (left) and Timothy Ford, dressed in casual clothes, were the top violin students at their school in Tonopah. (Lym.)

ROSE FORD. Rose was close to her father and occasionally went to the borax camp, where she is seen above relaxing with some of her father's coworkers. As she grew up, she became interested in American fashions and posed at left in a chic outfit with her father in the front of their house. With the exception of the Kee children, her friends were Euro Americans from different ethnic groups. After her parents' deaths in 1921 (Loy) and 1922 (William), she moved to San Francisco with her sister Bessie (1906–1995). They lived at the YWCA in Chinatown for a while and worked at the White House Department Store in downtown San Francisco. (Lym.)

EDUCATION. In 1877, the superintendant of schools in Nevada decided that Chinese American children could attend public school. In San Francisco, Chinese students had to attend segregated public schools. Pictured above in 1910, James Ford (second row, second to the right, next to Mary Connors, a lifelong friend) is with his eighth-grade class. Timothy and James lived at George Wingfield's home in Reno at the outbreak of World War I. They served in the military and eventually settled in Fresno, California. Seen in 1916, George Washington Ford (1906–1989) poses with his elementary school class far left, second row). In 1927, George married Ethel Chew of Winnemucca. Later, George taught the martial arts in Hollywood and was an advisor for the *Kung Fu* television series starring David Carradine. The children were the only Chinese students in their classes. (Below, CNHS.)

MYRTLE KEE. The Ford and Kee children were usually well dressed. At left, Myrtle poses in a fashionable sailor-inspired dress in 1912. When her mother moved the children to Virginia City where several members of the Yee clan were prominent members of the community, Myrtle and her siblings attended the fashionable and progressive Fourth Ward School (now a museum). Myrtle, the only Chinese child in the class, is seen (third row, fourth from the left) in the image below. The family returned to Tonopah around 1915 and then moved to Reno at the beginning of World War I. (At left, Kee; below, Fourth Ward School.)

FLORENCE KEE. In a school play in Tonopah, Florence Kee played the Powhatan princess Pocahontas (1595–1617). Her father had been a friend to the Native Americans living near Hawthorne. In 1915, Florence decided to marry Rudolph Espinoza of Basque descent. In 1861, Nevada passed a law barring marriages between Euro Americans and Chinese/Mongolians, and even cohabitation was regarded as a misdemeanor. Therefore, the couple decided to marry on the high seas. The marriage was reported in several newspapers, including the *San Francisco Chronicle* and *Elko Free Press* because the local sheriff had arrested them for violating the miscegenation law. Once the sheriff learned that the marriage took place with the blessings of Ah Cum, the newlyweds were released. The couple moved to Los Angeles, and in 1919 Florence died during the flu pandemic. (Kee.)

FRANK KEE. Frank and William Kee were photographed in their dress clothes in Tonopah sometime during the 1910s in the image above. They were the closest in age to George Ford and were frequent playmates. In 1915, Frank, on the far left in fourth row left in the picture below, attended the Fourth Ward School in Virginia City, but shortly after this photograph was taken the Kee family returned to Tonopah. His daughter Shirlaine Kee Baldwin, a resident of Berkeley, California, became the family historian and participated in the US Forest Service archaeological excavations of Chinese sites in Nevada. (Above, Kee; below, Fourth Ward School.)

AH CUM KEE AND DAUGHTER MAY KEE. Dressed in a fashionable outfit in the 1910s photograph above, Ah Cum Kee was well known in Tonopah and, later, in her new abode in Reno. Finding suitable mates for her children became problematic, but her daughter May was able to marry Dan Woo of Sparks, Nevada, and they raised their children in Nevada and, later, California. In the 1920 census for Sparks, there were only 38 Chinese people, only two of which were adult women, so the ratio of men to women continued to be high for men until the 1970s. (Kee.)

CHARLES KEE. In the image above, Charles Yuen Kee (1893–1977) stands in front of his horse and buggy in Tonopah. His father, Chung Kee, was very traditional and insisted that his oldest son, Charles, be sent to Guangdong, China, to find a bride. Unaccustomed to Chinese traditions, he was unhappy there and returned to Tonopah to sign up for the army during World War I. At left, Charles (left) poses with a fellow recruit. He never reunited with his wife and son after he left China, but he was close to his siblings and eventually became interested in tracing the family history. (Kee.)

SAM LEON FAMILY. Sam Leon (born in 1876 or 1879 and died in 1951) was a cook in Wabuska and later owned a home, saloon, hotel, and casino in Bodie, California. In the photograph at right, he is seen in Bodie. Around 1906, he married Daisy Benton (1881–1915), seen below, a Paiute. After Daisy's death, Leon felt that he could not raise their daughter Laura (born in 1910) by himself. He sent her to the Ming Quong Chinese Girls School in Oakland, California, and visited her regularly. In 1927, Laura lived with her maternal relatives in Schurz. Later, she graduated from nursing school, married, and had eight children, all of whom learned to speak some Cantonese and cook Chinese food. Laura and her children saw Sam regularly until his death in 1951 in Reno, where he worked as a cook. (At right, NPS; below, Juanita Pontoon.)

BERTHA COFFEE. Although the Chinese could not marry Euro Americans, they could marry Native Americans, Mexicans, and African Americans. Bertha Coffee, whose mother was Native American, lived with her Chinese father in Tonopah. She also was a longtime friend of the Kee and Ford children. (NHS.)

TONOPAH VICTORY PARADE. In 1920, the annual World War I victory parade in Tonopah was a big celebration, but the economy declined thereafter. (NHS.)

THE WAHS. Thomas (1871–1931) and Gue Gim (1900–1988) Wah, of Prince/Pioche, were married in 1916 in San Francisco. They are seen at right in front of their home. Thomas was born in Marysville, California, and returned with his aunt and uncle to China until he was an adult. He operated a boardinghouse and restaurant at the Prince/Caselton Mine and brought his new bride there. Gue Gim had immigrated in 1912, passing through Angel Island, as seen in the photograph below, and spent four years in San Francisco's Chinatown. She did not know English until she attended and graduated from the Prince School. After her husband's death, she met and became friends with Herbert Hoover, who had an interest in the nearby Castleton Mine. Wah's Cafe became famous in the region. She died in 1988 and was buried in Pioche. (At right, UNLV.)

Mrs. Huey and Daughter. Mrs. Chowsing Huey was born in 1873 and raised in California. She married Sing Huey Chow, but immigration officials gave him the name of Chowsing Huey. He owned a profitable steam laundry in Carson City, and she was one of Carson City's two midwives, taking care of Euro Americans and Washoe Native Americans. There was no physician in town in the late 1910s and 1920s. Her children were born in Carson City. During the Depression, the family relocated to Los Angeles. Hazel Huey was among the oldest, and because of her height and long legs, she became one of the early Chinese American Las Vegas showgirls in the 1950s. She later settled in Los Angeles. Even in her 90s, Hazel could still speak some Washoe that she learned as a child.

Five

RENO AND OTHER TOWNS

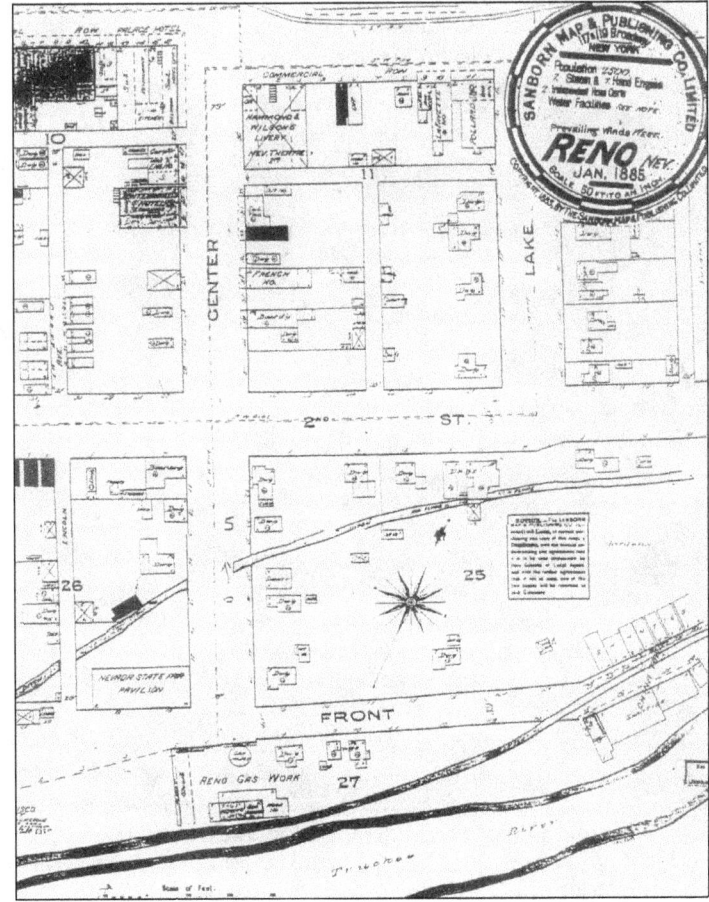

RENO, 1885. When the CPRR reached Reno, some of the Chinese settled in Reno and built their Chinatown along Front Street near Center Street. This Sanborn-Perris fire insurance map shows Chinatown in the lower right-hand corner. Chinatown expanded to include Lake Street as the Chinese population grew, but its central location angered city officials, who continually lobbied to burn Chinatown. In 1908, Chinatown was burned, and Euro Americans took over the site. (Sanborn map.)

LAUNDRY, 1904. One of the major industries for the Chinese population continued to be the laundry business. Tom's Laundry, located on Second Street between Center and Lake Streets in Reno, delivered laundry in his horse-drawn carriage. (NHS.)

OPIUM RAID. In 1906, an opium raid in Goldfield netted some beautiful pipes and lamps. According to local ordinances, no Chinese people could disembark from the train or live in Goldfield at this time. (NSM.)

RENO. In 1900, Reno's Chinatown had a Chinese gambling house opposite Cash's general store. Despite the fact that gaming was not legalized in Nevada until 1931, the Chinese had operated gaming establishments since the 1850s. Opium smoking and gambling were two of the vices that the anti-Chinese organizations decried. They also opposed the low wages paid to Chinese workers. The central location of Chinatown made it valuable property, and the anti-Chinese lobbyists tried various ways to take over the land. In 1908, Reno officials declared Chinatown a health hazard and burned it to the ground. Unprepared, over 150 Chinese were left homeless in the snowy winter and had to seek housing with friends and relatives elsewhere. (NHS.)

Group of Disconsolate and Homeless Chinese Viewing Ruins of Their Shacks After Work of Destruction Had Been Started by Dr. Robinson of Reno Board of Health. (Photo by Dann for the Gazette.)

MURDER. In 1921, Gee Jon (left) went to Mina with Hughie Sing (below) and killed a rival tong (secret brotherhood) member. Although they pleaded not guilty, they were convicted of first-degree murder. Gee was the first to be executed in the state by means of lethal gas. His case raised the issue of whether race was involved and if lethal gas was a cruel and unusual punishment. Hughie was born and raised in Carson City. He was given the death sentence for first-degree murder as well, but his attorney appealed. The public consensus was that he would have been charged with second-degree murder as an accomplice if he had been white. He won his appeal and became eligible for parole in 1930. Because he was such a good cook for the warden, he was not granted a parole until 1938. (NHS.)

WOMEN. Chinese women in the 1920s photograph at right and 1930s image below wore traditional Chinese dresses, which had become popular for special occasions and performances. Many of the dresses were made in China and sold in specialty shops or made by seamstresses in the American West. In 1920, the Reno census counted 630 males and 59 females for the Chinese, a ratio of 11 to 1, and in 1930 the number was 410 males and 73 females, a ratio of 17 to 1. In China, women were primarily homemakers and often had the support of family members and servants, but in the American West many of them were wage earners to supplement the income of their husbands.

Chinese Medicine. Since the 1860s, Chinese doctors treated the Chinese, Euro American, and Native American populations with herbs and acupuncture. In the early 1900s, Dr. Gee (or Yee) Tong (born in 1850, immigrated in 1871, and married in 1893) based his practice in Carson City but traveled to neighboring towns, including Tonopah. He advertised in the local papers announcing the dates of his presence in the towns. Other doctors followed his example. The remedies were usually imported from China, but because of the similarity between Chinese medicinal plants and Native American herbs, sometimes remedies were purchased locally. (At left, NSM; below, NHS.)

HERBS

The Sing & Kwan Herb Co.
The Famous Chinese Herbalists
WHEN OTHERS FAIL COME TO SEE US

CONSULTATION FREE

356 N. Virginia St. Phone 1226-W Reno, Nev.

HOURS:—9 to 12; 2 to 5; 7 to 8.   Sundays and Holidays by Appointment

DR. Q. S. WONG

CHINESE HERBS   CHIROPRACTOR
SPECIALIST   CHRONIC DISEASES

"ONLY ONE DR. WONG IN RENO"

TELEPHONE 422   315 GRANITE STREET   RENO, NEVADA

(1923) R. L. POLK & CO.'S

YEE FAMILY. In the 1930s, Dr. Tin Mon Yee opened his herb store on Lake Street in Reno. The Tin Mon Yee family grew. In the photograph above, Tin Mon Yee is standing and from left to right are Frances; Dr. Yee's wife, Wong Shee, holding infant Jessica; Peter; Poy; David; and Oy holding baby Layton. In 1948, Dr. Peter Yee married Helen, and the family gathered for the auspicious event. In the image below are Annie, Herbert, Lilly, Layton, Frances, Harry, Helen, Peter, Mary, Rita with Cheryl, David, Tin Mon, Wong Shee, Poy, and Oy. (Yee.)

CHINESE WOMEN. Most Chinese women did not work in public places, but occasionally they were employed at restaurants. The woman above is seen working in a saloon in 1920 and, like many Chinese women of this generation, has brought her child with her to workplace. However, parties sometimes required special dresses, and in the festive occasion seen below that took place sometime around 1930, the women are wearing traditional Chinese cheongsam dresses. (Above, NHS; below, Shoong.)

EUREKA. On July 4, 1928, Washoe County treasurer Daniel Dunkle visited longtime resident and Eureka community leader Wong Och Lem. Eureka, known for mining and smelting ore, was established in 1864. In 1880, with a Chinese population of 481 out of the 4,207 residents, most of the Chinese were cooks, laundrymen, and domestic servants. There also were five physicians, two miners, and nine woodchoppers. In 1900, the Chinese population was only 29 with one physician. By 1920, the census counted only nine Chinese, including one merchant, three retirees, and five in the restaurant business. Chinatown, which was located across the street from the local newspaper office and, therefore, often in the news, gradually disappeared, and in 1994 only a single Chinese American restaurant, seen below, remained. (At right, NSH.)

ELKO. Since its establishment in 1868, Elko has remained a major transportation center. By 1920, the 34 Chinese locals were primarily in the restaurant business. The Shanghai Cafe was one of the popular restaurants.

YUP HOME IN KAIPING, 1930. Like many Chinese, California-born Hen Yup of Lovelock built a home of a Western design in the overseas Chinese community in Kaiping, Guangdong, and his brother constructed an identical one next door. (Yup.)

HENRY YUP WEDDING AND FAMILY. Hen Yup's son Henry, who was born in China and immigrated at the age of 12, was sent to Kaiping to find a bride in 1937. Henry married Dorothy Wong (right), but because of immigration regulations he was forced to leave his wife and newborn daughter, Carole, behind in the family home. After serving in World War II, he returned to Kaiping to see his wife and daughter, now eight years old, and other relatives, as shown in the image below. In 1941, he was able to bring his wife and daughter to Nevada, and the family later grew to include four boys and three more girls, all of whom were noted for their academic and professional achievements. (Yup.)

Yup. Henry Yup, owner of four restaurants in the Reno area, including the Sun Café, and a community leader, wanted to build a home for his large family in the prestigious southwest section of Reno. Residential restrictions made this difficult, but he overcame the problems. Like many prominent Chinese Americans like the Wing Fong family in Las Vegas, he built a Chinese-inspired home there. He also graced the cover of the Reno telephone book one year, thus, becoming a celebrity. Yup and his wife were fond of celebrating Christmas and displayed decorations inside and outside of the house. (At left, Yup.)

CHINESE FREEMASONS, C. 1950, AND THE YUPS. By the 1950s, the Chinese population in Reno had declined, and many buildings, including the formerly impressive brick Chinese Freemason lodge, were abandoned. In 1957, the lodge was demolished. Henry Yup, along with several other Chinese American leaders, fought for the city to reimburse the Chinese community, and the funds were used to build a Chinese pavilion in a nearby Rancho San Rafael Park, Reno's largest county park. (Above, NHS; at right, Yup.)

GAMING. The Chinese enjoyed gambling, and gaming houses could be found in almost all of Nevada's Chinatowns. In 1905, Ching Sang offered faro at his casino in Reno. In the 1907 photograph above, a Chinese man is playing faro with Euro American men. In 1921, card games became legalized, and in 1931 gambling was legalized. From 1952 until 1973, William Fong (1920–1982), seen below, operated the New China Club at 260 North Lake Street in Reno. Open to people of all races, the casino attracted Euro American blue-collar workers. Because of racial discrimination, African Americans were not allowed in major casinos until the 1960s. All of the Chinese dealers at the New China Club had to join the Hop Sing Tong, a fraternal organization with its national headquarters in San Francisco. The delicious Chinese American food was one of the attractions to the New China Club. (NHS.)

NEW CHINA CLUB. Joe Louis is pictured above with William and Ann Fong in 1960. To show his appreciation for his African American dealers and customers, William Fong established a scholarship fund for African Americans to attend the University of Nevada, Reno and raised some of the money through golf tournaments. Many African American dealers that went on to work in major Nevada casinos acknowledge the training that he provided them. He also sponsored the annual Chinese New Year parade in Reno from 1952 until 1973, as well as several Hop Sing Tong national conventions. (Above, NHS; below, NSM.)

EXCHANGES AND ADOPTIONS. After the recognition of the People's Republic of China in 1979, educational and cultural exchanges increased. Lucia You attended graduate school in the United States and taught the Chinese language at the University of Nevada, Reno. Later, she became the director for the University of Shanghai Yanchang campus for University Studies Abroad Consortium, headquartered in Reno. She is pictured below in 2010 with Zhang Wen, a Chinese language instructor who did her graduate work in Florida. In 1994, many American citizens began adopting Chinese children, primarily girls as a consequence of the one-child policy that the Chinese government instituted in 1980. By 2008, there were 3,909 adoptions. These young girls, adopted by Reno and Carson City schoolteachers, gathered together for special events, such as the dedication of a plaque commemorating the site of Carson City's Chinatown.

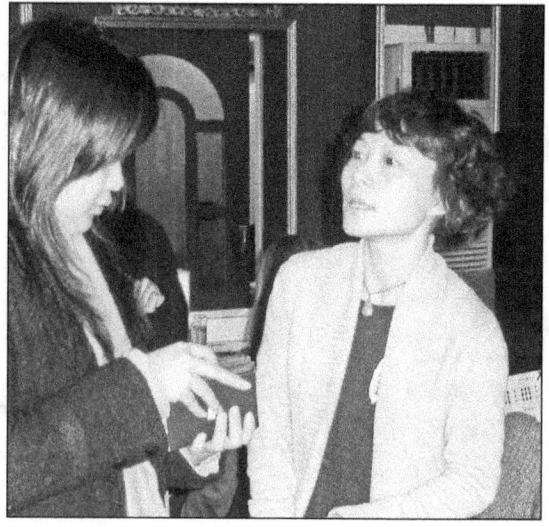

Six
ENTERTAINMENT AND LATER DEVELOPMENTS

CHINESE MUSICAL INSTRUMENTS. The Chinese brought their love of music to the American West. During the 1870s in Tuscarora, the Chinese band played to welcome the winning sports team. In the 1920s and 1930s, Chinese musicians traveled to different venues to perform. (NSM.)

THUNDERBIRD. The Thunderbird Hotel and Casino, which was the fourth hotel on the Las Vegas Strip, was open from 1948 until 1992. Shortly after World War II, several hotels featured Asian performers, and the Thunderbird was known for its China Doll Revue, with a cast of 35, in the late 1950s. The billboard at left from 1958 features Hawaiian-born Frances Fong, also seen below, who went on to work in Hollywood until 2000. Sisters Bo Ling and Bo Ching also performed in Las Vegas and then joined the Screen Actors Guild in Hollywood until their retirement.

OTHER ENTERTAINERS. Gia Mo, at right, wife of Jerry Terheyden Jr., was 23 when she was part of the Magic Carpet Revue at the new Dunes Hotel in Las Vegas in 1955. Daughter of a Chinese Episcopalian bishop, she left Kunming, China, in 1949, graduated from Carnegie Tech, and performed in the Broadway production of *The King and I*. She is one of the many who made her entertainment debut in Las Vegas. Male performers, seen below, also performed in the entertainment industry. (At right, UNLV.)

CASINO. Chinese-owned casinos were established in Las Vegas beginning in 1931. From 1954 until 1956, Hawthorne-born William Kee (1903–1956), seen at left, operated the El Cid Club in Las Vegas that was owned by the Mar family of Fresno, California. A fire started in the casino not long after the African American Moulin Rouge Hotel and Casino was also severely damaged by fire. Kee suffered a fatal heart attack after he successfully put out the fire at the El Cid. Other Chinese-owned casinos included the China Mint (Reno, 1960–1963), Chinese Pagoda (Sparks, 1946–1948), Chinese Village (Las Vegas), Town Hall Casino (Las Vegas), Siena (Reno), and the Eureka Casinos (Las Vegas and Mesquite). In the photograph below, Moon Ong, the first Chinese American dealer on Fremont Street in Las Vegas, began working in 1958. He opened the door for Asian American dealers. (At left, Kee; below, Ong.)

SAM YET. Sam Yet (died 1932) was born in northern Nevada to an Irish mother and Chinese father. He married a Euro American woman, settled in Searchlight, Nevada, and eventually owned five prosperous mines, which he sold for $45,000 in 1928. (UNLV.)

CHINESE CALLIGRAPHY. A sample of Get Chor Chan's calligraphy from the 1940s demonstrates the skilled hand of a traditional Chinese scholar.

NATIONAL DOLLAR STORE. Joseph Shoong (1879–1961) was born in Zhongshan, Guangdong province, in 1879. Immigration officials reversed his Chinese name of Chow (last name) Shoong (first name). He immigrated in 1899. Beginning in 1916, he started a chain of stores known as the National Dollar Stores (which son Milton headed after his death), was active in urban development and real estate, and participated in the stock market to become one of the early Chinese American millionaires. By 1959, the National Dollar Store had 54 branches in California, Hawaii, Arizona, Washington, Utah, and Nevada (one in Reno, one in Las Vegas). He died in 1961, and a public park in Las Vegas was named in his honor. The Las Vegas store seen below was located on Fremont Street and opened before its rival, JC Penney, located across the street. It closed in the mid-1970s. (At left, Shoong-Lee; below, NSMLV.)

Shoong Family. The Shoong family (right) are, from left to right, son Milton, wife Rose, mother Chow Wong Shee, daughters Bette (back), and Doris (front), and Joseph Shoong. They are photographed here on board the ship wishing safe travels before Chow Wong Shee's departure back to China. By traveling first class, Chinese immigrants and visitors did not have to undergo the rigorous immigration procedures as those traveling in other classes. The family poses (below) in front of their family car. (Shoong-Lee.)

101

MARRIAGES. In 1959, Nevada repealed its 1861 miscegenation law, thus allowing Chinese, like Alvin Woon On Chung, to marry a Caucasian, Ellen Day (at left). No longer were interracial couples subject to arrest, which had been the case of Florence Kee and her Hispanic husband. In 2000, Nevada ranked fifth in the nation with the number of ethnically diverse marriages. The repeal of the Chinese exclusion acts in 1943 allowed Boulder City resident and restaurant owner Fred Lee to bring a bride from China, and their wedding reception was celebrated by many prominent Caucasian friends (below). The law allowed more Chinese women to immigrate, but a balanced ratio of men to women was not reached until 1980. (At left, SK Chung.)

CHINESE RESTAURANTS. The Chinese Pagoda occupied a historical 1901 former hotel but was forced to close in around 1950. Although the Chinese were prohibited by law from working on the Hoover Dam and other public projects, the Chinese knew that the workers and tourists in Boulder City needed food. Fred's Café, owned by Fred Lee, and Harry's Cafe, also known as the Boulder City Cafe, opened in the 1950s. Below, in 1958, Harry Won and his wife, Toy King Won, are seen inside of the restaurant. (Above, NHS; below, Ong.)

WANDA ONG AND SONS. By the 1970s, Chinese Americans began to participate in occupations that had not been open to them earlier in the 20th century. Wanda Ong, daughter of Harry Won of Boulder City, is seen above with her friend Frank Buckley in front of the courthouse she worked in during the 1970s. Other Chinese Americans became managers of casinos and hotels, government workers, and office holders. Wanda's two sons, Kane Ong (front row, second from the right) and Kenneth (front row, third from the left), were probably the first Chinese American firefighters in Nevada, as seen below during their graduation ceremony in 1977. (Ong.)

LAS VEGAS ORGANIZATIONS. The Las Vegas branch of the Chinese Consolidated Benevolent Association (CCBA) honored T.W. Chow, the consul general for the Republic of China in San Francisco in the 1960s. From left to right are Sui Mon Fong and Harry Won (co-chairs of the CCBA), Chow, Wing Fong, mayor pro-tem Hank Thornby, and University of Nevada, Las Vegas Pres. Roman Zorn. Since the beginning of the establishment of Chinatowns in Nevada, Chinese New Year celebrations were held and usually included the non-Chinese population. In Las Vegas during the 1970s, the Ying On Merchants and Labor Benevolent Association, a fraternal society with non-Chinese members working toward the promotion of businesses, invited the community to join them in this major festival, as seen below. Here, the lion dance is being performed in downtown Las Vegas where their original headquarters was located. (Above, Ong.)

HIGH SCHOOLS. The civil rights movement in the mid-1950s opened the doors for Chinese Americans to participate more in school and community organizations; in occupations, including law, education, medicine; and other activities. Many achieved new goals in high schools. Above, Kathy Chang of Las Vegas High School (second row, far left) became a member of the prestigious Rhythmettes in 1964. At left, Walter M. Solomon, born and raised in Las Vegas, won the 2011 Woodie Flowers Regional Award for mentoring the Preuss Charter School robotics team. (Above, UNLV.)

AMERICANS BORN IN CHINA. Beginning in the late 18th century, American traders went to China, and a few of them married Chinese women. American missionaries also constituted a substantial number who settled in China, along with diplomats and businessmen. In the 1940s, American servicemen also lived in China, some bringing their wives. Pam and her younger sister Stephanie Moore were born and spent their early years (to 1949) in Shanghai under the watchful eye of their amah, Ah Hong. Later, Stephanie settled in southern Nevada and was a member of the Nevada Ballet Theatre as a regular dancer and then as a character dancer, with one of her most memorable roles as Mother Ginger in *The Nutcracker*. When China opened to American tourists in the 1980s, Stephanie Myers was able to visit her birthplace. (Myers.)

OVERSEAS LINKS. Like many Chinese with relatives in the American West, the Wai Seng Cheung family of Hong Kong sent annual Christmas photographs to relatives in order to reinforce clan ties.

NEWSPAPER. By the 1970s, several Chinese-language newspapers with a focus on local and international news were published in Las Vegas for the growing Chinese population and, thus, supplemented those published in California.

Seven
ACCOMPLISHMENTS AND CONTRIBUTIONS

LAS VEGAS CHINATOWN. Although several locations have served as Las Vegas's Chinatown since 1905, it was not until 1995 when Taiwan-born James Chen opened Chinatown Plaza, anchored by 99 Ranch Market, on Spring Mountain Road. With a pan-Asian flavor, Chinatown has become permanent and flourishing.

CHINESE NEW YEAR. The celebration of the Chinese New Year, which is based on the lunar calendar, is held in Las Vegas's Chinatown and has become a large community event lasting an entire day with performances, food stalls, crafts, and activities. This celebration began in Nevada in the 1850s and was a part of the many Chinatown activities through the centuries. The photograph above is one of several lion dances performed in 2007. Although performers for the lion dances were brought in from other locations, Las Vegas eventually developed its own troop with the Lohan School of Shaolin. Below are some of the colorful lion heads used by the performers in the festival.

MOON FESTIVAL. The celebration of Chinese festivals was not limited to Chinese sponsorship. In 2010, the Springs Preserve in Las Vegas hosted its first Autumn Moon Festival, and thousands turned out for the entertainment, food, crafts, and activities. A beautifully crafted dragon decorated one of the areas of the preserve, Chinese lanterns were hung throughout the park, and the attendees were of many ethnicities and ages.

ACUPUNCTURE. Acupuncturist Chester Chin (1920–1999), born in China, was a 13-year resident of Las Vegas. He served on the Board of Oriental Medical and had a thriving acupuncture practice, which involved the insertion of needles, use of herbal remedies, and dietary requirements. His colleague, Dr. Yee Kung Lok of Las Vegas, was instrumental in the legalization of acupuncture and oriental medicine in 1973, making Nevada the first state on the mainland to officially recognize this ancient method of medical treatment. Chester is seen above with his wife celebrating Chinese New Year at the Chinese Garden Restaurant. Acupuncture is an ancient Chinese treatment involving the insertion of needles into certain points in the body, as demonstrated in the image below. (Above, UNLV.)

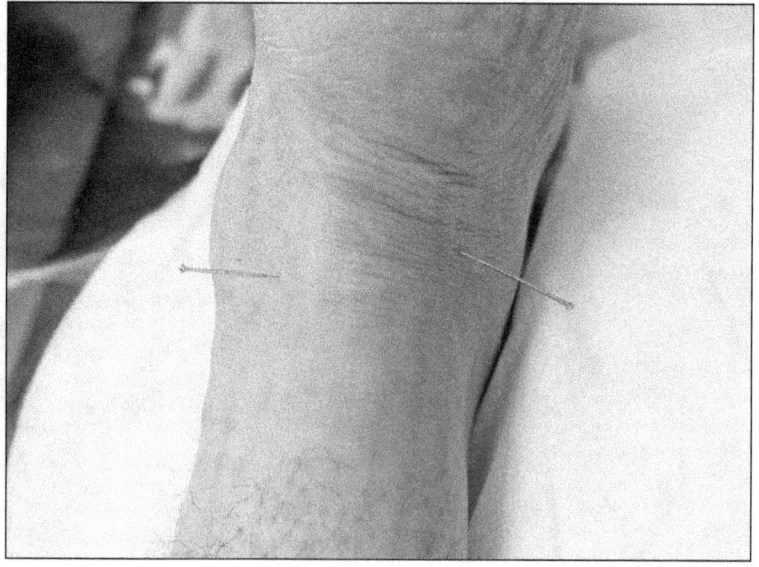

WING AND LILLY FONG. Arizona-born Lilly Fong (1925–2002), the first Chinese American public schoolteacher in Clark County, served as president of the Association of American University Women in Nevada. She served on the Board of Regents from 1974 until 1984. A university building on the University of Nevada, Las Vegas campus was named in her honor. Wing Fong (1925–2005), Lilly, and their children, Kenneth and Susan Fong, are in the photograph below in their Las Vegas home in 1977. The community recognized the couple as one of the first 100 important people shaping southern Nevada. Wing graduated from Woodbury University in Los Angeles. He married Lilly Hing, and they moved to Las Vegas. Wing established Fong's Garden in 1955, founded the Nevada State Bank and a savings and loan in Las Vegas, and was active in a real estate development.

DEDICATION. In 1992, the Wing and Lilly Fong Elementary School was opened in honor of the community leaders. Above, at the dedication ceremony with Wing and Lilly Fong are Cheryl Lau, JD, and US senator Richard Bryan. Cheryl Lau was born in Hawaii in 1944 and served as Nevada's secretary of state from 1992 until 1995—the first Asian American to hold a high statewide position. She unsuccessfully ran for governor in 1994 and the US Congress in the second district in 1996. She has served as the general counsel to the US House of Representatives and currently serves as a judge pro tempore in the Carson City Municipal Court system. She is very active in Reno and Carson City community activities. (Below, UNLV.)

ARCATA. From supporting America's ventures into space to the flight lines and front lines of the US military, Arcata Associates has played a key role in the aerospace industry and won awards for its work. The photograph above shows founder Buck Wong breaking ground in 1990 for the company in North Las Vegas with Sen. Richard Bryan (center) looking on. Wong also served as president of the North Las Vegas Chamber of Commerce. When Buck Wong retired as president of Arcata Associates, his two children, Lawrence "Timothy" and Nancy, photographed with their parents, took over and expanded Arcata Associates, relocating the company in Las Vegas. Timothy and Nancy are active in the Las Vegas community and have served on the boards of numerous community organizations.

RICHARD TAM. Tam (1916–1999) is seen in 1990 receiving the Silver State Award from Fred Albrecht, university alumni relations director, for his contributions. The alumni building was named in his honor. (UNLV.)

TIFFANY LEE. In 1998, Tiffany Lee (born 1986), a second-generation Nevadan, is leading the Meadows School Chinese New Year Parade at Caesar's Palace in Las Vegas. The children concluded the parade with songs sung in Chinese.

STUDENT ACHIEVEMENTS. Beth Au, a graduate of Las Vegas High School, assisted in the cultural exchange program that brought dinosaur skeletons from Sichuan, China, to the Las Vegas Chinatown. She is photographed above with Sen. Harry Reid. Beth went on to receive her master's degree from the University of California, Los Angeles. Chinese American students have been known for their high educational achievements. In the 1970 and 1980 census, more Chinese students completed a four-year college education than any other group. At right is Alexander Solomon, who is partially of Chinese ancestry. He was presented with the Presidential Scholar Award by Pres. George W. Bush in Washington, DC, in 2005 for his academic achievements and community service. Only two students are selected from each state every year. Alexander graduated from Harvard University with honors in biochemistry in 2009.

THEODORE AND DORIS LEE. Doris Shoong Lee, the youngest daughter of Joseph Shoong, resides in Las Vegas with her husband, Theodore B. Lee. They have been very active in the Las Vegas community and were the founding sponsors of the Las Vegas Philharmonic. They established the first professorial chair in the University of Nevada, Las Vegas Boyd Law School and actively supported the UNLV Foundation. Doris also has served as chair of the Asian Art Museum in San Francisco. Theodore served on Harvard University's Board of Overseers and the Board of Governors of the East West Center in Honolulu, Hawaii. Their two sons, Greg and Ernest, also are active in the community. (Shoong-Lee.)

GREG LEE. Since 2002, Gregory T.H. Lee, JD, has been the president of the Eureka Hotel and Casino in Mesquite and vice president of Urban Land of Nevada, a real estate company with offices in Las Vegas and San Francisco. A graduate of Harvard University and the University of Southern California Law School, he is very active in the community, serving on numerous boards and as president of the Young Presidents Organization.

MICHAEL CHANG. During his tennis career, Michael Chang (born 1972) lived in Henderson. In 1989, at age 17, he was the youngest player to win a Grand Slam singles title at the French Open. He was inducted into the International Tennis Hall of Fame in 2008. (Chang Foundation.)

OCA. Shan O-Yuan, at left, served as the second president of the Organization of Chinese Americans (OCA), a national political empowerment and civil rights group founded nationally in 1973. With 44 chapters, one was established in Las Vegas in the 1990s. Other groups were formed, including the Asian Chamber of Commerce in 1986, the Las Vegas Chinese American Chamber of Commerce in 1997, and a local branch of the Chinese American Citizens Alliance (founded in San Francisco in 1895) in 2002. These organizations work on immigration and discrimination issues, political empowerment, civil rights, and professional and business interests. The OCA held its national conference in Las Vegas in 2005, and Buck Wong and his daughter Nancy attended along with Wayne and Sadie Tanaka, as seen in the photograph below. Asian Americans, representing the fastest growing minority in the state, constituted 6.6 percent of Nevada's population in 2009.

Louie. Like many others, Chinese Americans have retired to Nevada from many parts of the United States. Daniel Louie Jr. (PhD in plant physiology, UCLA) and his wife, Esther, a retired school administrator, were both born in California and moved to Las Vegas. They continued to be active in the community, which earned them both (on separate occasions) the International Ambassador of Goodwill Award from the Lions Club International. Among their many contributions was fundraising for the University Medical Center Burn Center and working toward the establishment of an Asian bank, both in Las Vegas.

Judges. Several Chinese Americans have served as judges in Nevada. In 2011, Jerry Tao (JD, George Washington University), the son of Taiwanese immigrants and former lobbyist and government employee in Washington, DC, became a Clark County District judge.

LEAF AND LIU. Recent emigrants from China have made contributions to the arts. Born in Guangdong, William Leaf translated his Chinese family name of Yip (leaf) as his American family name. He joined the University of Nevada, Las Vegas faculty in the early 1970s and became a nationally known print maker and artist. He curated several art exhibitions, including one of Chinese American artists. Pictured above, he is standing in front of one of his creations. Born in Fuling, China, Stephen Liu, PhD, seen below, taught English at Southern Nevada Community College from 1973 until 2001. He became internationally famous for his poetry in Chinese and English. He was the first Nevadan to receive the National Endowment for the 1981–1982 Arts Fellowship in Creative Writing, as well as numerous other awards.

VICTOR KWONG. Victor H.S. Kwong (PhD, University of Toronto, 1979) joined the University of Nevada, Las Vegas Physics Department and developed an innovative ion storage facility to study low-energy collisions between ions and neutral atoms and molecules. The aim of his work is to understand the role of these collisions in the energy redistribution in fusion and astrophysical plasmas.

FRED LEE. State architect Fred Lee designed a variety of public buildings throughout the state beginning in the 1990s. Among them were the renovation, expansion, and redesign of the John Wright Hall on the University of Nevada, Las Vegas campus that was completed in 2005 and is seen here in 2010.

PHYSICIANS. Chinese Americans practicing Western medicine became prominent in the 1960s. Among the many was psychiatrist Elisabeth Chan Small, MD, photographed at left, who graduated from the UCLA School of Medicine in 1960. After doing her residency and practicing in Boston, she relocated to Reno and joined the University of Nevada, Reno School of Medicine faculty in 1982, achieving emeritus status in 1995. James Lum, MD (1929–2010), seen below, was a radiologist who graduated from Yale School of Medicine and was a partner in the first professional corporation in the Silver State that later was known as Desert Radiologists. Other early physicians in Las Vegas included Hawaii-born Clifford C.H. Lee, MD, an allergist, and Boulder City–born Fred D. Lee, a gynecologist.

DIVERSITY. During the decade between 2000 and 2010, the number of multi-ethnic people in Nevada increased by 50 percent, and the number of Asian Americans increased by 116 percent. Author and University of Nevada, Las Vegas special collections librarian Su Kim Chung, seen at right (back row, left), is one of the growing numbers in this category and is seen with her parents, Alvin and Kelly Chung, and sister Su Lon Chung. Born and educated in Reno, Liane Lee worked in Washington, DC, and then returned to Nevada to continue her work in politics while she pursued her master's degree in public administration. In the March 2010 photograph below, she is featured in Las Vegas City Hall highlighting the importance of diversity. The sign, E Pluribus Unum, Latin for "out of many, one," is appropriate for the growing diverse Nevada population. (Above, SK Chung.)

MASTER E-MAN. Traveling Daoist priests still perform ceremonies in Nevada. Master E-Man, born in Taiwan and living in Southern California, is seen performing a Daoist ceremony during the installation of good luck lions at Caesar's Palace on the Las Vegas Strip in 2010.

ASKING HEAVEN. Although the Chinese in Nevada have been forgotten by many, artist Joan Giannecchini found herself fascinated by their history and lifestyle and recently completed this work, entitled *Asking Heaven*, which exhibited in the Northeastern Nevada Museum. Zhi Lin also became fascinated by the history of the Chinese in America and worked on a project in 2007 entitled, "Invisible and Unwelcomed People: Chinese Railroad Workers."

BIBLIOGRAPHY

Chan, Sucheng and Madeline Y. Hsu, *Chinese Americans and the Politics of Race and Culture.* Philadelphia: Temple University Press, 2008.
Chang, Iris. *The Chinese in America: A Narrative History.* New York: Penguin Books, 2004.
Chen, Shehong. *Being Chinese, Becoming Chinese American.* Urbana, IL: University of Illinois Press, 2002.
Chung, Sue Fawn. *In Pursuit of Gold: Chinese American Miners and Merchants in the American West.* Urbana, IL: University of Illinois Press, 2011.
Daniels, Roger, *Asian America: Chinese and Japanese in the United States since 1850,* Seattle: University of Washington Press, 1988.
Hing, Bill Ong. *Making and Remaking Asian America through Immigration Policy, 1850—1990.* Palo Alto: Stanford University Press, 1993.
Hsu, Madeline. *Dreaming of Gold, Dreaming of Home: Transnationalism and Migration between the United States and South China, 1882–1943.* Palo Alto: Stanford University Press, 2000.
Kwong, Peter and Dusanka Miscevic. *Chinese America: The Untold Story of America's Oldest New Community.* New York: New Press, 2005.
Lai, Him Mark. *Becoming Chinese American: A History of Communities and Institutions.* Walnut Creek, CA: AltaMira Press, 2003.
Lee, Erika. *At America's Gates: Chinese Immigration during the Exclusion Era, 1882–1943.* Chapel Hill: University of North Carolina Press, 2003.
McClain, Charles J. *In Search of Equality: The Chinese Struggle Against Discrimination in Nineteenth-Century America.* Berkeley, CA: University of California Press, 1994.
Tong, Benson. *The Chinese Americans.* Westport, CT: Greenwood Press, 2000.
Tsai, Henry Shih-shan. *The Chinese Experience in America.* Bloomington, IN: University of Indiana Press, 1986.
Yung, Judy. *Unbound Feet: A Social History of Chinese Women in San Francisco.* Berkeley, CA: University of California Press, 1995.
Zhao, Xiaojian. *Remaking Chinese America: Immigration, Family, and Community, 1940–1965.* New Brunswick, NJ: Rutgers University Press, 2002.

Visit us at
arcadiapublishing.com

www.ingramcontent.com/pod-product-compliance
Lightning Source LLC
Chambersburg PA
CBHW081417160426
42813CB00087B/1474